POP-OUT & PAINT

HORSE BREEDS

Create Paper Models of 10 Different Breeds

Cindy A. Littlefield

Storey Publishing

Have You Herd?

Imagine if you could have any horse you wanted — a buckskin Quarter Horse, a palomino Tennessee Walker, a silver-dappled Shetland Pony, perhaps. Better yet, what if you could round up a whole stable full of horses to call your own?

Crafted from punch-out paper bodies and embroidery floss or yarn manes and tails, the make-your-own model horses in this book are striking stand-ins for the real thing. And they're surprisingly easy to create. For example, simply dab on a little paint with a soft sponge and you've got a horse with a dappled or roan coat. Or use a cotton swab to apply spots on an Appaloosa's blanket.

So turn the page and meet the herd: **eight horses, a pony, and a pair of foals** that include a variety of distinctive breeds and coat colors. Then follow the step-by-step directions to create the models shown in the book. Or mix and match the different painting techniques and manes and tails to create your very own one-of-a-kind herd.

When you're done, check out page 38 for instructions on how to use cardboard and paper to construct **a tabletop stable** with Dutch doors that open and close. Then round up some scrap paper and a few household materials to make the **mini grooming tools, show ribbons, and other cool equine accessories** starting on page 40. Once you've used the templates in this book, you can use the leftover pages as stencils for tracing and cutting out more horse shapes from heavy cardstock.

CONTENTS

Meet the Horses

4
The Rocking Tennessee Walker

5
The Thundering Thoroughbred

6
The Shaggy Shetland

7
The Mighty Morgan

8
The Flashy Friesian

9
The Sassy Saddlebred

10
The Quick Quarter Horse

11
The Colossal Clydesdale

12
The Splashy Appaloosa

13
The Elegant Arabian

Make the Models

See how to make a halter and lead rope on page 47.

Sandpaper serves as a riding trail or road.

Performing Palominos

Palominos have been cast in some of Hollywood's most memorable equine roles. Roy Rogers's famous stallions, Trigger and Trigger Jr., were palominos. The latter was a Tennessee Walker who could dance and perform a host of clever tricks.

Mr. Ed, another talented television star, could lift a ladder, carry a bird in a cage, and pull covers over himself while pretending to go to sleep.

THE TENNESSEE WALKER IS ONE SMOOTH MOVER. It has a gentle, rocking-horse canter, a gliding slow walk, and the unique running walk for which it is most famous. During the running walk, the Tennessee Walker nods its head and swings its ears as it reaches a whopping walking speed of up to 12 mph. With its comfortable gaits and good nature, this breed is well suited to both casual trail riding and flashy show performances. Typical coat colors are chestnut, bay, and palomino.

YOU WILL NEED

* Template on pages 49–52
* White cotton embroidery floss
* Black, white, and tan paint

HOW TO MAKE THIS HORSE

1. **HOOVES (PAGE 20):** Paint them black.

2. **WHITE MARKINGS (PAGE 22):** Paint the blaze and stockings.

3. **SHADING:** See the diagram on page 26 for details.

4. **DETAILS (PAGE 28):** Retrace the eyes, nostrils, and mouth with black. Add a white glint to the eyes. Add shading to the ears.

5. **MANE & TAIL (PAGE 31):** Add a long, flowing mane and tail. Leave a gap at the top of the neck where the mane is often trimmed short to show off the arched neck. Follow step A to make the forelock.

The Thundering **Thoroughbred**

See how to make jumps on page 43.

SIX STRIDES AND 2½ SECONDS — that's how long it takes a Thoroughbred racehorse to go from a standing start to running 40 miles per hour! Agile, long-legged, and lean, this breed can really go the distance, not only on the racetrack but also in cross-country steeplechase races, where horses sail over fences, ditches, and hedges at a full gallop. Typical Thoroughbred coat colors are bay, black, and chestnut; white markings are common.

Sky High

In 1944, a Thoroughbred named Faithful was retired from racing and trained to jump. Competing under his new Chilean name of Huaso, he set a new world record by clearing an 8-foot, 2-inch fence!

YOU WILL NEED

* Template on pages 53–56
* Reddish brown cotton embroidery floss
* Reddish brown, black, and white paint

HOW TO MAKE THIS HORSE

1. HOOVES (PAGE 20): Paint them black.

2. WHITE MARKINGS: Paint the blaze and stockings (page 22).

3. MUZZLE (PAGE 23): Sponge a little diluted brown paint on the muzzle.

4. SHADING: See the diagram on page 26 for details.

5. DETAILS (PAGE 28): Retrace the eyes, nostrils, and mouth with black; add a white glint to the eyes. Add shading to the ears.

6. MANE & TAIL (PAGE 31): Add the mane and tail and trim them neatly. Follow step A on page 33 to make the forelock.

The Shaggy Shetland

Cotton batting makes a pretty winter scene.

Pony Power

In the 1800s, when more and more coal was being used to fuel engines and furnaces, thousands of Shetland Ponies were used in mines in England and the United States. Working long days alongside the miners, these short-legged, chunky-bodied "pit ponies," as they came to be called, provided the muscle power to pull the coal carts through the underground shafts.

ONE QUICK LOOK AT THE SHETLAND PONY and you may wonder, *Is there really a pony under all that mane?* The answer of course is *yes* — and it's quite a pony. Brave, spirited, and playful, the Shetland is used for riding and driving and is strong enough to pull up to twice its weight. The Shetland's coat can be most any color, including pinto and dappled gray, which is fairly common.

YOU WILL NEED

* Template on pages 57–60
* White cotton yarn
* Black, white, and gray paint

HOW TO MAKE THIS HORSE

1. **COAT (PAGE 16):** Sponge dapples all over the body.

2. **HOOVES (PAGE 20):** Paint them white.

3. **WHITE MARKINGS (PAGE 22):** Paint the feather on the legs.

4. **MUZZLE (PAGE 23):** Sponge on white paint.

5. **SHADING:** See the diagram on page 26 for details.

6. **DETAILS (PAGE 28):** Retrace the eyes, nostrils, and mouth with black; add a white glint to the eyes. Add shading to the ears.

7. **MANE & TAIL (PAGE 31):** Add a thick, long mane and tail. Follow step A on page 33 to make the forelock.

The Mighty Morgan

See how to make a hay bag on page 44.

Wood shavings or sawdust makes great bedding.

No DOUBT YOU'VE HEARD THE SAYING "Good things come in small packages." In the horse world, the Morgan proves the point. Although they tend to be on the small side, Morgans have muscular hindquarters and they step proudly and willingly with their heads and tails held high, making the breed a great choice for riding and driving. Morgans are usually brown, black, chestnut, or bay, but can be lots of other colors except pinto. They may have small white markings.

YOU WILL NEED

* Template on pages 61–64
* Black cotton or pearl cotton embroidery floss
* Black, white, and gray paint

HOW TO MAKE THIS HORSE

1. **HOOVES (PAGE 20):** Paint them dark gray.

2. **BLACK POINTS (PAGE 21):** Sponge black paint onto the lower legs and muzzle.

3. **SHADING:** See the diagram on page 26 for details.

4. **DETAILS (PAGE 28):** Retrace the eyes and mouth with black and the nostrils with gray; add a white glint to the eyes. Add shading to the ears.

5. **MANE & TAIL (PAGE 31):** Add a full, flowing mane and tail. Follow step A on page 33 to make the forelock.

Go Figure!

The Morgan breed descends from a single sire named Figure. Despite being just 14 hands tall, he won nearly every race he ran, and once even hauled a giant log that a draft horse couldn't budge. Figure's speed was passed on to his great-grandson, a horse called Ethan Allen 50, who became the world's fastest trotting stallion and inspired the classic weathervane horse image seen spinning above many barn roofs today.

The Flashy **Friesian**

See how to make a halter on page 47.

See how to make a halter on page 47.

Winter Mustache

Meet a Friesian horse in the summertime and you might not notice that it has a mustache. That's because the act of grazing naturally "shaves" it off. No kidding! Come winter, though, the hair on the Friesian's upper lip can grow long enough to curl into a full handlebar-style mustache.

WITH ITS MUSCULAR BODY, long wavy mane, full leg feathers, and quick high-stepping trot, the Friesian is the perfect mix of strength and style. Little wonder it was the horse of knights, moving with grace and ease while carrying a man in full armor. Today, the breed's elegance and its friendly nature make it a popular carriage and dressage horse. Although the coat color originally included gray and chestnut, nowadays it is always black, generally without markings other than a small star.

YOU WILL NEED

* Template on pages 65–68
* Black cotton embroidery yarn or floss
* White, black, and gray paint

HOW TO MAKE THIS HORSE

1. **HOOVES (PAGE 20):** Paint them dark gray.

2. **HIGHLIGHTS:** See the diagram on page 26 for details.

3. **DETAILS (PAGE 28):** Retrace the eyes, nostrils, and mouth with dark gray or near black; add a white glint to the eyes.

4. **MANE & TAIL (PAGE 31):** Add a long, thick mane and tail. Follow step A on page 33 to make the forelock.

The Sassy **Saddlebred**

See how to make jumps on page 43.

THANKS TO ITS SPRINGY STEP AND FIERY ENERGY, the American Saddle-bred is often called the "Peacock of the Show Ring." Some Saddlebreds perform two gaits in addition to the walk, trot, and canter — the "slow gait," which is like a regular walk but much quicker, and the "rack," in which the horse snaps its knees and hocks high into the air while traveling up to 35 miles per hour! Saddlebreds come in almost all colors and have long, flowing manes and tails.

YOU WILL NEED

* Template on pages 69–72
* White and dark brown cotton embroidery floss
* Black, dark brown, pink, and white paint

HOW TO MAKE THIS HORSE

1. **COAT (PAGE 18):** Pencil on a pinto pattern and fill it with paint.

2. **HOOVES (PAGE 20):** Paint them dark gray.

3. **MUZZLE (PAGE 23):** Sponge on diluted pink paint.

4. **SHADING:** See the diagram on page 26 for details.

5. **DETAILS (PAGE 28):** Retrace the eyes, nostrils, and mouth with brown; add a white glint to the eyes. Add shading to the ears.

6. **MANE & TAIL (PAGE 31):** Add a long, flowing mane and tail, mixing white and brown floss. Follow step A on page 33 to make the forelock.

Pinto or Paint?

Although these two words are often used interchangeably, there's a difference. *Pinto* refers to a distinctive coat color in which the body is white with irregular black, brown, or palomino patches. A *Paint* is an actual breed with a stocky build and strict bloodline requirements. So, although all Paints are pintos, not all pintos are Paints.

The Quick **Quarter Horse**

See how to make a lead rope on page 47.

See how to make a lead rope on page 47.

The Dun Factor

At first glance, you might think a dun and a buckskin are one and the same. Take a closer look and you'll see that although both have base coats that range from a golden cream to tan, the dun's has a sooty tinge. Even more telling is the fact that duns have dark dorsal stripes running from the poll to the dock of the tail, and most buckskins do not.

HORSE RACING HAS BEEN POPULAR in America since colonial times. When English horses were bred with the small-but-speedy Chickasaw Indian horses, the result was a new type of compact, muscular horse that could sprint like the wind — a fact proved in quarter-mile races held right on the main streets. Later, when pioneers headed west, the Quarter Horse took quickly to ranch life. Today it is a top performer in Western riding competitions. Quarter Horses can be any solid coat color.

YOU WILL NEED

* Template on pages 73–76
* Black cotton embroidery floss
* Black, white, and gray paint

HOW TO MAKE THIS HORSE

1. **COAT (PAGE 17):** Leave as is, or sponge on a very thin layer of a lighter or darker tan for a mottled look.

2. **HOOVES (PAGE 20):** Paint them dark gray.

3. **BLACK POINTS (PAGE 21):** Sponge black paint onto the lower legs and muzzle.

4. **WHITE MARKINGS (PAGE 22):** Paint the blaze and fetlock.

5. **SHADING:** See the diagram on page 27 for details.

6. **DETAILS (PAGE 28):** Retrace the eyes, nostrils, and mouth with black; add a white glint to the eyes. Add shading to the ears.

7. **MANE & TAIL (PAGE 31):** Add the mane and tail, trimming them neatly. Follow step B on page 33 to make the forelock.

The Colossal **Clydesdale**

See how to make a lead rope on page 47.

A roll of cork serves as footing for a paddock.

A FULLY GROWN CLYDESDALE CAN MEASURE UP TO 18 HANDS HIGH — over 6 feet at the withers — so it's no surprise that the foals weigh as much as 180 pounds at birth and gain at least 4 or more pounds a day for their first few months. Originally bred for farming and coal mining in Scotland, these gentle giants are still used for ecofriendly farming and logging. Clydesdales are typically black or brown, often with white on the underbelly. The breed's long, silky "feather" or "feathering" on its legs makes it instantly recognizable.

Five-Pound Shoes?

When a horse weighs a ton or more, it's bound to have big feet. In fact, a draft horse's hooves are about twice the size of a Thoroughbred's, and each of its shoes can weigh five pounds. Even so, the Clydesdale is a graceful mover, lifting its hooves high enough off the ground that spectators can see the soles of its feet.

YOU WILL NEED:

* Template on pages 77–80
* Medium-weight soft-textured light and/or dark brown yarn
* White, tan, and black paint

HOW TO MAKE THIS HORSE

1. HOOVES (PAGE 20): Paint them tan.

2. WHITE MARKINGS (PAGE 22): Paint the blaze and stockings.

3. MUZZLE (PAGE 23): Sponge on diluted black paint.

4. SHADING: See the diagram on page 27 for details.

5. DETAILS (PAGE 28): Retrace the eyes, nostrils, and mouth with black; add a white glint to the eyes. Add shading to the ears.

6. MANE & TAIL (PAGE 31): Add a short, fuzzy mane and tail. Follow step B on page 33 to make the forelock.

The Splashy Appaloosa

See directions for making this barn on page 38.

See how to make this bench, some grooming tools, and a tool box on pages 40–42.

See directions for making this barn on page 38.

See how to make this bench, some grooming tools, and a tool box on pages 40–42.

Snappy Appys

Horses with colorful spotted coats were prized around the world long before the Appaloosa made its debut in North America. There are horse images in ancient cave paintings of south-western France that are covered with dots.

FEATURING **BOLD SPOTS**, speckles, and blankets, the Appaloosa is one breed not likely to get lost in the herd. These strong, athletic horses were bred by the Nez Percé Indians, who wanted a horse that was fast enough to ride in buffalo country. With their muscular build, Appaloosas are well suited to ranch work, trail riding, and Western sports. In addition to their flashy coats, they have distinctive mottling on their muzzles as well as striped hooves.

YOU WILL NEED

* Template on pages 81–84
* Brown cotton embroidery floss
* Brown, white, black, pink, and gray paint

HOW TO MAKE THIS HORSE

1. **COAT (PAGE 19):** Follow the directions to create the blanket and spots.

2. **HOOVES (PAGE 20):** Paint them dark gray with lighter stripes.

3. **WHITE MARKINGS (PAGE 22):** Paint the blaze and socks.

4. **MUZZLE (PAGE 23):** Sponge on pink paint; use the tip of a paintbrush to dab on brown mottling.

5. **SHADING:** See the diagram on page 27 for details.

6. **DETAILS (PAGE 28):** Retrace the eyes, nostrils, and mouth with black; add a white glint to the eyes. Add shading to the ears.

7. **MANE & TAIL (PAGE 31):** Add a sparse mane and tail and trim the mane short. Follow step A on page 33 to make the forelock.

The Elegant **Arabian**

See how to make these ribbons on page 44.

See how to make this wooden pallet on page 45.

THE **ARABIAN IS ONE OF THE OLDEST AND MOST BEAUTIFUL BREEDS,** and there are some great myths about its origins. In one tale, the breed is said to have received spirit from the North wind, strength from the South, speed from the East, and intelligence from the West. Myth or not, the Arab is well known for these qualities and many more. Easily recognized by its dished face and arched neck, the Arab has influenced many modern breeds. Its fine, silky coat can be bay, black, brown, chestnut, or gray.

YOU WILL NEED

* Template on pages 85–88
* White and silver cotton and/ or rayon embroidery floss
* Black, white, gray, and pink paint

HOW TO MAKE THIS HORSE

1. **COAT (PAGE 16):** Sponge on a gray roan coat.

2. **HOOVES (PAGE 20):** Paint them black.

3. **MUZZLE (PAGE 23):** Sponge on pink paint; add a light layer of gray.

4. **SHADING:** See the diagram on page 26 for details.

5. **DETAILS (PAGE 28):** Retrace the eyes, nostrils, and mouth with black; add a white glint to the eyes. Add shading to the ears.

6. **MANE & TAIL (PAGE 31):** Add a full, flowing mane and tail. Follow step B on page 33 to make the forelock.

Shades of Gray

Did you know that there's no such thing as a white Arabian horse? True white horses have pink skin, but Arabians have black skin. So Arabian horses that appear white are considered gray. In fact, gray horses of all breeds are usually born black or brown and then turn lighter and lighter as they age.

STEP 1. Collect Your Supplies

Now that you've met the horses, it's time to put together a herd of your own. Besides the templates included in this book, you'll need a few basic craft supplies and items from around the house. Once you've gathered the materials on the list, just follow the easy step-by-step directions.

FOR PAINTING THE BODY

* Acrylic craft paints (see breed page for specific colors)
  * black
  * dark brown and/or reddish brown
  * white
  * off-white
  * pink
* Craft paintbrushes in several sizes
* Sponge (synthetic craft sponges work especially well)
* Cotton swabs for painting Appaloosa spots
* Pencil
* Paper plate or disposable plastic lid to mix paint on
* Paper towels

FOR CREATING A MANE & TAIL

* Embroidery floss and/or yarn (see breed page for specific colors)
  * black
  * white
  * dark brown
  * reddish brown
* Scissors

FOR MAKING A STAND

* Regular paper clips
* Pliers for bending the paper clips

FOR PUTTING IT ALL TOGETHER

* Glue (a good-quality glue stick or tacky glue for gluing the paper template halves together and glue dots for attaching the manes, tails, and paper clip stands)
* Pinch-style clothespins or large paper clips (to hold the template halves together while the glue dries)

EXTRAS & FINISHING TOUCHES

* Fine-tipped, black permanent marker
* Silver marker for adding horseshoes
* Glue sealer, such as Mod Podge, for sealing the templates after you've painted them (optional)

TIP: You can mix paints to make other colors. For example, black and white make gray, whereas brown and white make tan. Experiment to see how much of each color you need to get the color you want.

It's a good idea to cover your work surface with newspaper, waxed paper, or a piece of cardboard. Besides keeping paint off the table, it makes cleaning up a snap.

Use a fine-tipped brush for adding facial details.

Use medium brushes for painting pinto spots and markings, and for spreading tacky glue.

Use a broader brush to apply glue sealer to the painted templates.

Use a sponge to create a roan or dappled coat, or to add black points.

STEP 2. Paint Your Horse

What's great about making paper horses is that you don't have to be an artist to do it. It's amazing how quickly a few strokes or dabs of paint can transform a plain template into a horse or pony with plenty of personality. Time to get started!

Popping Out the Templates

Choose the horse you want to create and pop out the pair of matching templates from the middle of the book. (Afterward, you can use the template pages as stencils for tracing more horse bodies onto colored card stock or poster board.)

One template is for the side of the horse facing you and the other is for the side that faces away. Make sure that they face each other while you paint them so they will line up right when it's time to glue them together.

> **TIP:** If you make a mistake, you can start over on the other side, but don't forget to flip both templates so they'll still line up correctly.

CORRECT
(nose to nose)

INCORRECT
(nose to tail)

Painting the Coat

Sometimes coat color is part of the breed (Friesians are always black, for example). Some breeds, like the Quarter Horse, can be a variety of solid colors. In other breeds, like the Saddlebred, any color goes, including pinto splotches! And then there's the Appaloosa, which is known for its colorful spots and splatters in a huge range of patterns.

Sometimes solid coat colors are accented with other colors. Examples of this are dappling (overlapping spots and patches that blend into the base color) and roaning (a mixture of dark and light hairs that create an overall speckled look).

* **IF YOU'RE PAINTING A SOLID-COLOR HORSE,** you can go right to page 22 and start adding any markings you like.

* **IF YOU'RE PAINTING A SPOTTED OR DAPPLED HORSE,** the techniques for the different coat patterns are on the next few pages.

Shetland Pony

Other breeds that might have dapples are the Arabian, the Quarter Horse, the Saddlebred, the Tennessee Walker, and the Thoroughbred.

FACT: Dapples often develop as a foal grows up and fade later in life.

Delightful Dapples

Dapples are overlapping spots and patches that blend into the base color. To make a dappled coat, sponge on the paint just thick enough to leave some bigger blotches among the speckles. The holes in the sponge will create a dotted effect in these blotches.

* **To make the dappled gray Shetland Pony,** use white, off-white, or light gray paint on top of the base color. Sponge-paint the whole body.

* **Dapples aren't just for grays** — brown horses can have dapples too. For a dappled bay, use darker brown or dark gray on top of the brown base coat.

* **Dapples can also appear** just on the rump or the barrel of a horse.

Arabian

Among other breeds that can have roan coloring are the Quarter Horse, the Thoroughbred, and the Clydesdale.

FACT: Unlike gray horses, which are born dark and lighten with age, roans stay the same color their whole lives.

Roan Tones

A roan coat is a mixture of dark and light hairs that produce an overall speckled look. To create a finely speckled roan coat, blot your sponge on scrap paper or a paper towel until most of the paint is removed before sponging the template.

For a roan, you can sponge-paint as much or as little of the body as you like. The Arabian shown here has just a few random patches of speckling on its head, neck, flanks, and legs.

* For a **silver gray roan** like this, use a medium gray over the white base coat.

* For a **blue roan,** swirl a tiny bit of black paint into some white and sponge it onto a black horse.

* For a **strawberry roan,** stir a touch of reddish brown or pink into white paint and sponge it onto a medium or light brown horse.

HERE'S THE BASIC TECHNIQUE:

1 Tear off a piece of sponge and put a little paint on a paper plate or plastic lid.

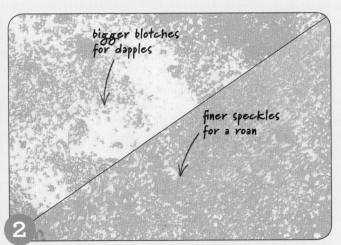

bigger blotches
for dapples

finer speckles
for a roan

2 Practice sponge-painting on scrap paper for a few minutes. Lightly press the dry sponge into the paint and then blot the paper to see what it looks like. This will give you a good idea of the amount of paint you'll need on the sponge to get the effect you want — bigger blotches for dapples or finer speckles for a roan.

3 When you paint the template, it's a good idea to start with a thin coat. You can always top it with more layers if you want the paint to be thicker.

Tennessee Walker

Splashy Pinto Patches

What's great about creating a pinto horse is that you can make the patches and spots look however you want, plus the patches can be black or any shade of brown. It's up to you!

Other breeds that often have pinto coloring are the Saddlebred and the Shetland. Thoroughbreds can be pinto — it's rare, but accepted by the breed registry.

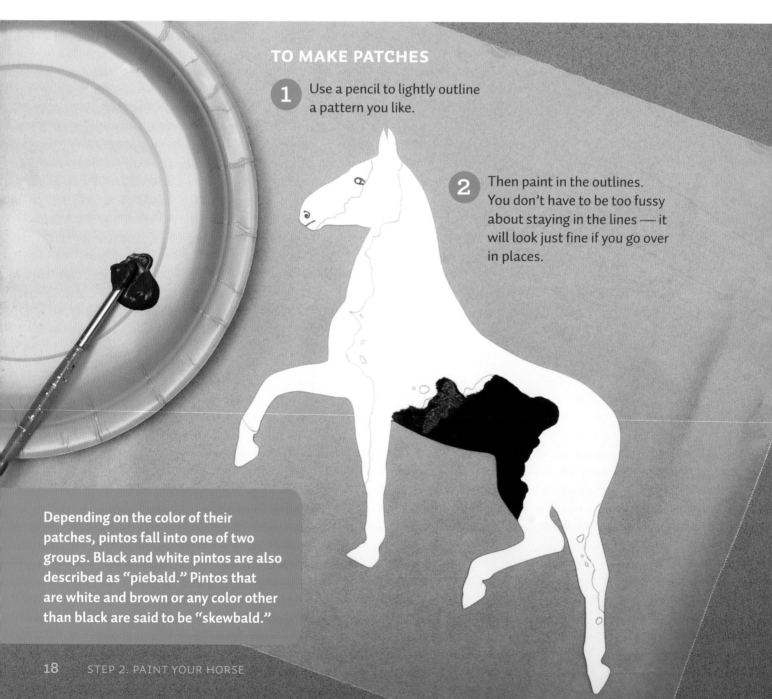

TO MAKE PATCHES

1 Use a pencil to lightly outline a pattern you like.

2 Then paint in the outlines. You don't have to be too fussy about staying in the lines — it will look just fine if you go over in places.

Depending on the color of their patches, pintos fall into one of two groups. Black and white pintos are also described as "piebald." Pintos that are white and brown or any color other than black are said to be "skewbald."

Appaloosa

Appy Blankets and Spots

Appaloosa (or Appys, as they're affectionately known) come in just about every color you can imagine and in a whole bunch of different spot patterns. This one, called a "blanket with spots," is especially striking. Plus, it's a blast to paint!

FACT: Spotted horses can be found all over the world and are prized in many cultures for their striking colors.

TO CREATE A BLANKET WITH SPOTS

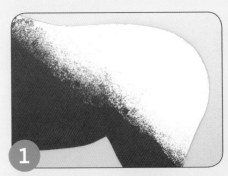

1 Sponge white or off-white paint onto the horse's rump to create the Appaloosa's blanket.

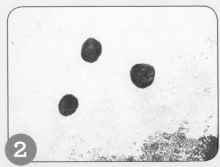

2 Use a cotton swab to dab brown spots on the blanket.

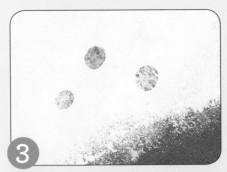

3 Sponge a second coat of white or off-white over the spots. Not too thick — you should be able to see the spots underneath when you're done.

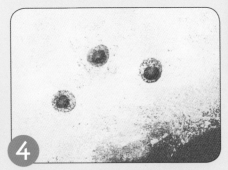

4 Dab slightly smaller brown spots right on top of the first ones. This creates the distinctive rings or "halos" that often outline an Appaloosa's spots.

TIP: Let the paint dry between each step.

Painting the Hooves

Generally, a hoof is close in color to the skin on the leg just above it, called the coronet. The coronet is the thin band of tissue just above the hoof, and the hoof grows from it. What if a horse has three dark legs and one white sock? You guessed it — chances are that three of its hooves will be black or dark gray and one will be off-white or light tan or beige.

To paint the hooves, lightly draw a pencil line across the top of each hoof, and then brush on paint to fill them in.

TIP: Keep in mind that the hair at the coronet band will extend down a bit over the hoof. So, rather than painting a perfectly smooth line at the top of the hoof, use the tip of your paintbrush to apply the paint a little unevenly.

For a white leg, paint the hoof a light color.

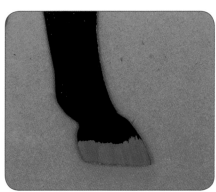

For a black leg, use dark gray for the hooves. This will create just enough contrast to keep the hooves from blending in with the legs.

If you want to "polish" your horses' hooves for a horse show, use a darker color as pictured on many of the horses in this book.

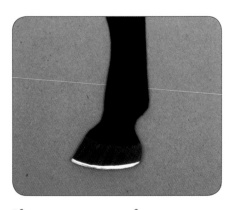

If you want to get fancy, you can add horseshoes. Simply use a silver marker to color the very bottom edge of each hoof.

What about Stripes?

This usually happens when a horse has dark spots on its coronet bands. Striped hooves are a common trait of Appaloosas and other breeds with spotted skin. To create stripes, start by painting each hoof black or dark gray. Then dip a small straight-edge brush in medium or light gray paint and brush straight down from the coronet band. Add one or two more stripes to complete the hoof.

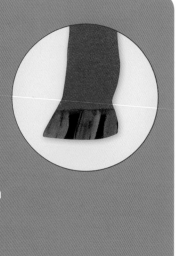

Adding Black Points

Are you making a bay or a buckskin? If so, it's time to sponge-paint on its black points. Remember, the points are the legs, muzzle, and tips of the ears (the mane and tail come later!).

Morgan

Quarter Horse

TO ADD POINTS

1 First pull off a small piece of your sponge and use it to practice dabbing black paint on scrap paper. Using a smaller piece makes it easier to control where the paint goes.

2 Start with the legs, going from the tops of the hooves up and over the knees and hocks.

3 Sponge a little black onto the horse's lower nose and mouth.

TIP: You don't need much paint — you can always add more but it's hard to remove once you've applied it.

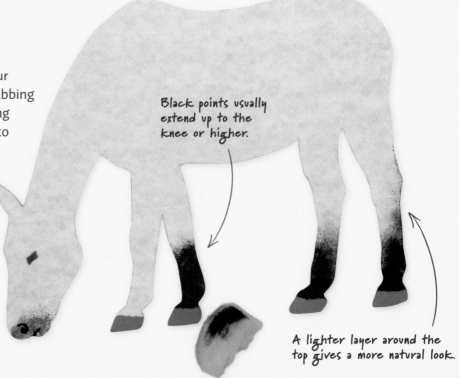

Black points usually extend up to the knee or higher.

A lighter layer around the top gives a more natural look.

Markings on Points

Horses with black points can also have white markings on their legs and faces. If you decide to paint a white marking on top of a black point, you may have to apply several coats of white until you can't see through to the darker color. See the next page for more about making white markings.

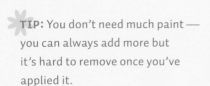

Making White Markings

Many horses have some combination of white markings on their faces and/or legs. These markings are there from the time a horse is born and are one of the features that let us tell apart individual horses with the same coat color.

Here are samples of facial and leg markings you may choose to put on your paper horses. It's fun to come up with a unique combination.

TO MAKE WHITE MARKINGS

1 Lightly pencil the markings on the template.

2 Use a paintbrush to fill in the areas with white paint.

Feather or Not?

Horses often have a tuft of hair growing from the backs of their lower legs and ankles, or fetlock joints. It's called "feather," and with some breeds, such as the Shetland Pony, it can be extra long and shaggy.

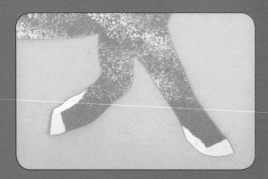

To add feather to a paper pony, brush a thick coat of white or off-white paint on the back edge of each leg from the midpoint of the cannon bone to the top of the hoof.

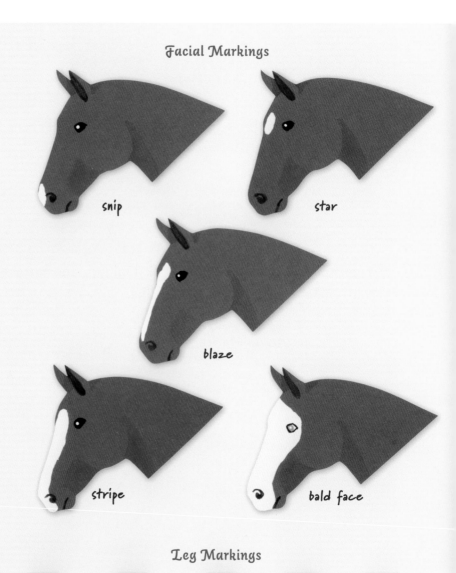

Facial Markings

snip

star

blaze

stripe

bald face

Leg Markings

coronet

pastern

fetlock or boot

sock

stocking

Tinting the Muzzle

If you're making a horse with black points (Quarter Horse or Morgan), you've already painted the muzzle black. Sometimes a horse without points will have a muzzle that looks darker or lighter than the rest of its face. That's because the hair around the mouth and nostrils tends to be thinner and more velvety than the rest of the coat, and so the skin is more visible.

To tint the muzzle, dilute a little bit of paint with water and then brush or sponge the diluted paint onto the muzzle.

Once the paint dries, use a marker or paint and a fine-tipped paintbrush to recolor the mouth and nostril lines.

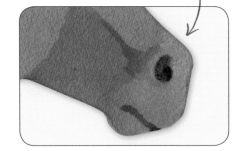

For a horse with a gray coat or light markings on its muzzle (Arabian, Shetland, Saddlebred, Clydesdale, Tennessee Walker), dilute pink paint or a lighter shade of the coat color with an equal amount of water.

For a horse with a black coat (Friesian), dilute white paint with an equal amount of water to highlight the muzzle, if you'd like.

For a horse with a light brown or chestnut coat (Thoroughbred, Appaloosa), mix an equal amount of water with a paint color that's close to the base coat.

An Appy's Mottled Muzzle

If you're making an Appaloosa, you'll want to add some mottling. This speckling around the mouth, nose, and eyes is one of the breed's distinctive traits.

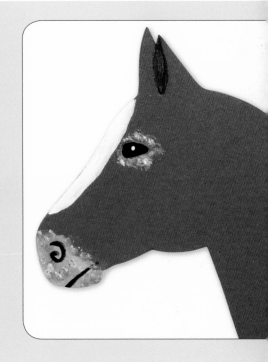

1. Begin by brushing or sponging diluted pink paint on the muzzle.

2. Then use the tip of a thin paintbrush to randomly add small dots of brown and tan or off-white paint to the pink area.

3. If you like the way it turns out, let the paint dry and then recolor the mouth and nostril lines. If not, simply sponge brown paint over the muzzle to cover it up and start again.

4. When you're done with the muzzle, use the same paintbrush and colors to add a spattering of dots around the eyes. While you're at it, use the very tip of the brush to add a tiny glint of white to each eye itself.

Creating Shading and Highlighting

This is the step that will really make your paper horse look three dimensional and more lifelike. Before you start, think about how different parts of the body create shadows on other parts. See the chart below for tips on shading and highlighting for each model.

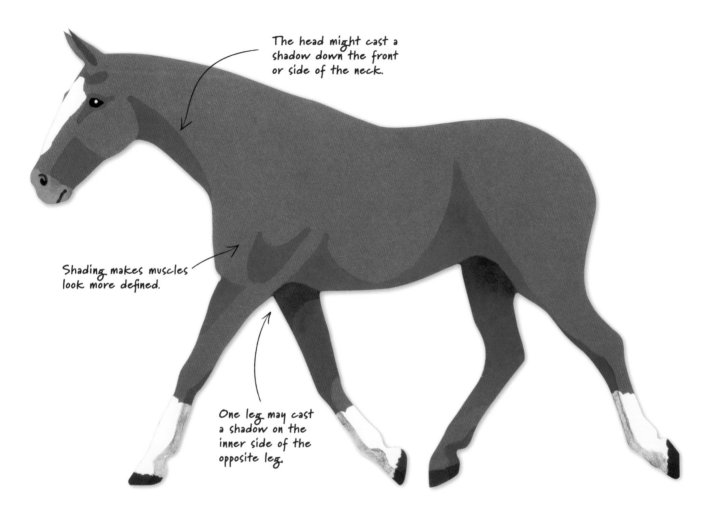

The head might cast a shadow down the front or side of the neck.

Shading makes muscles look more defined.

One leg may cast a shadow on the inner side of the opposite leg.

How exactly do you create these shadows or reflections? All you need is a little watered-down paint. The color you use depends on the color of the horse. Here's how it works for the models in this book.

BREED	PAINT COLOR
Appaloosa, Clydesdale, Morgan, Saddlebred	Black
Tennessee Walker	Tan (slightly darker than coat color)
Arabian, Quarter Horse, Shetland, Thoroughbred	Medium gray
Friesian	Light gray or white

TO CREATE SHADOWS AND HIGHLIGHTS

1 Dilute the paint with an equal amount of water, enough so you can see through it when you brush it on the horse. Practice first on scrap paper and if it's still too thick, add a little more water. Remember, you want it to look like a shadow instead of a patch of paint. If it turns out too light, just mix in a little more paint.

2 When you're ready to start shading, rinse your paintbrush clean. Then dip the brush in plain water and lightly wet the first area you plan to shade. This will give you a good idea of how the shading will look on the horse.

3 If the dampened area seems too big or small or mis-shapen, just let the paper dry and try again. If it looks good, go right over the area with diluted paint. This method of wetting the paper first also helps keep the paint in the spot you want.

4 Continue this way until you've finished all the areas you want to shade.

TIP: What if a shaded spot or highlight turns out a little too big or dark? If you act quickly, you can "erase" or at least lighten the painted area by blotting it with a piece of paper towel.

A Dark Horse
If a horse has a really dark coat, like the black Friesian, you might not notice the shadows so much. Instead, you're more likely to see highlights, which are the places on the body that reflect light (see detail in circle).

Shading and Highlighting Guide

Use these diagrams as a general guide for shading or highlighting on the horse you're making. Some areas will be a little lighter and others will be a little darker; just make the paint a tiny bit thicker for the darker parts. Don't worry about following the markings exactly — the idea is to give your model a little more depth and liveliness.

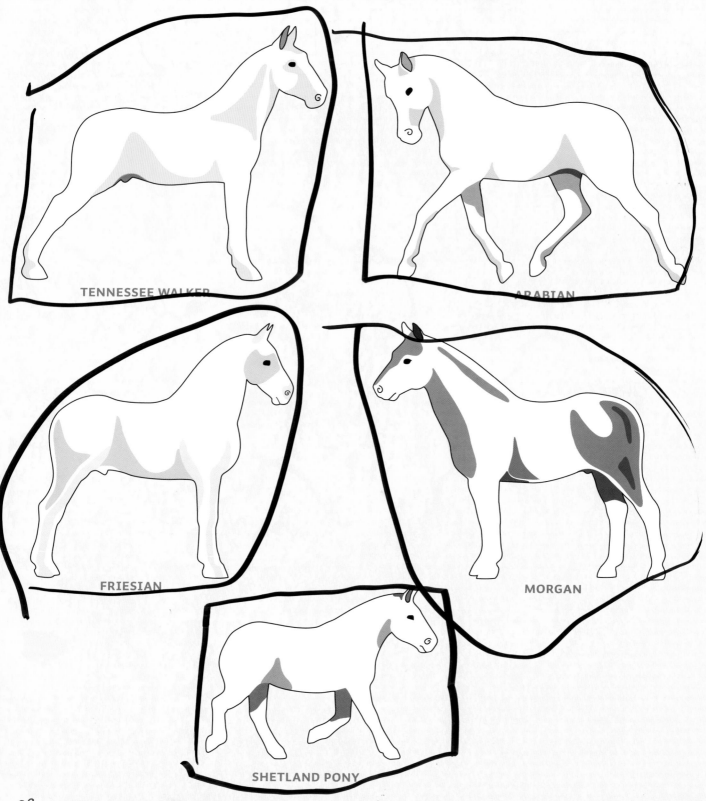

TENNESSEE WALKER

ARABIAN

FRIESIAN

MORGAN

SHETLAND PONY

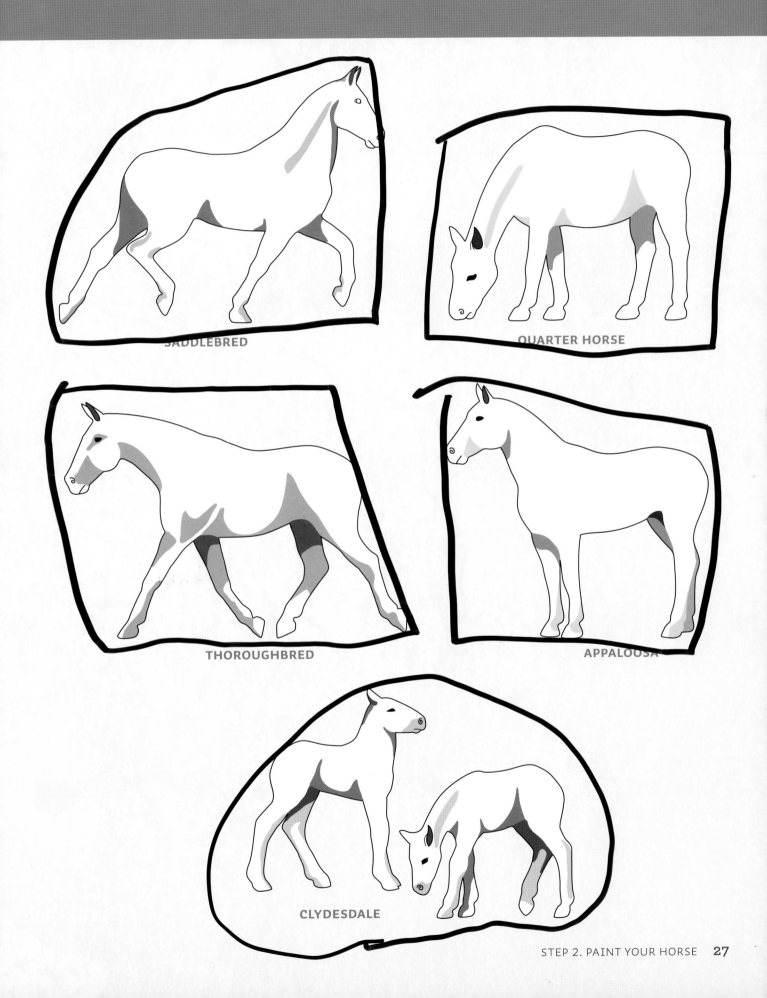

SADDLEBRED

QUARTER HORSE

THOROUGHBRED

APPALOOSA

CLYDESDALE

Detailing the Eyes, Ears, and Nostrils

After the shading is done, you'll want to give the facial features and ears a final touch-up to make your horse look even more lifelike.

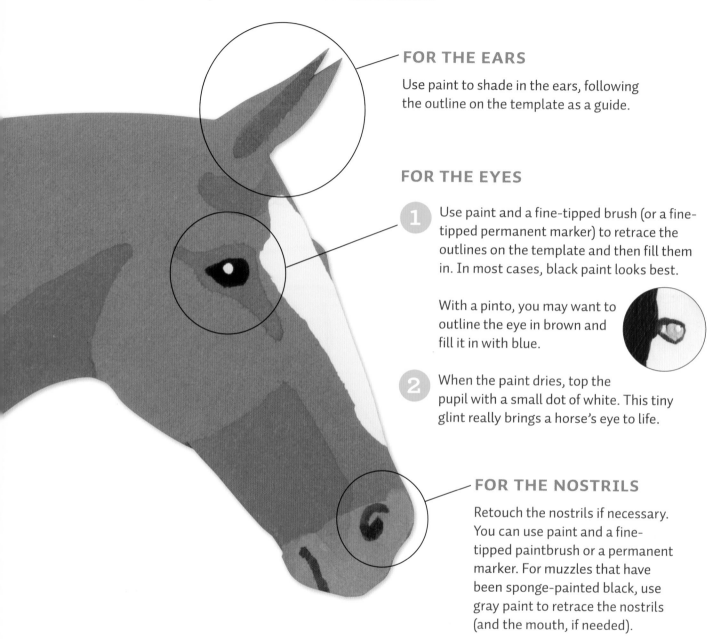

FOR THE EARS

Use paint to shade in the ears, following the outline on the template as a guide.

FOR THE EYES

1. Use paint and a fine-tipped brush (or a fine-tipped permanent marker) to retrace the outlines on the template and then fill them in. In most cases, black paint looks best.

   With a pinto, you may want to outline the eye in brown and fill it in with blue.

2. When the paint dries, top the pupil with a small dot of white. This tiny glint really brings a horse's eye to life.

FOR THE NOSTRILS

Retouch the nostrils if necessary. You can use paint and a fine-tipped paintbrush or a permanent marker. For muzzles that have been sponge-painted black, use gray paint to retrace the nostrils (and the mouth, if needed).

Protect Your Model

To add a little sheen to your horse's coat and to protect it from moisture, consider coating the painted template pieces with a clear-drying, nontoxic, water-based glue sealer. Use a clean soft paintbrush to apply the sealer. It's a good idea to try it on scrap paper first to see how it spreads.

Details on the Ears

When you're painting the shaded part of the ear, think about the direction it's facing. On ears that face forward, the shaded portion resembles a thin teardrop because you're looking at the side of the ear, not directly into it. For ears are turned more to the side, the shaded shape is fuller because you are looking straight into the opening. The close-up pictures below will help you see how your horse's ears should look.

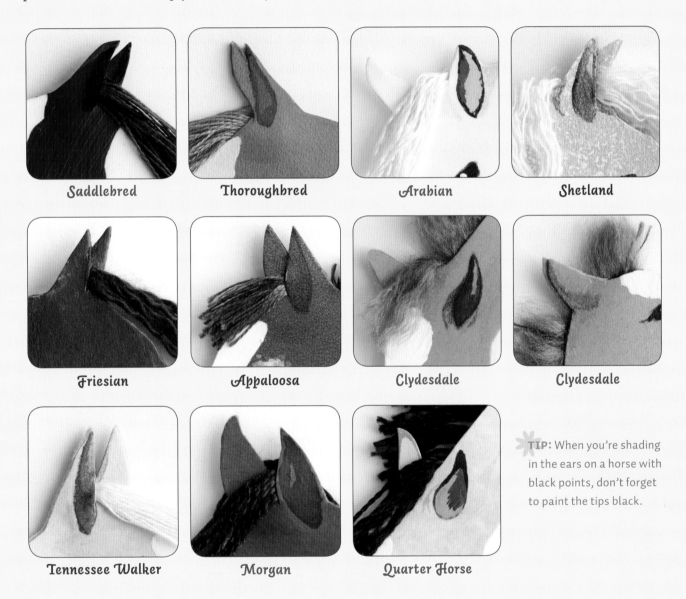

Saddlebred

Thoroughbred

Arabian

Shetland

Friesian

Appaloosa

Clydesdale

Clydesdale

Tennessee Walker

Morgan

Quarter Horse

TIP: When you're shading in the ears on a horse with black points, don't forget to paint the tips black.

STEP 3. Add the Mane and Tail

Without a doubt, a horse's mane and tail are its most eye-catching features — and the ones horse fans most love to groom and style. Manes can be left long and natural, shortened and thinned, braided or banded, or clipped close to the neck. Tails can be long or short as well, and sometimes they're even tied into a big knot to keep them from getting too muddy or tangled.

Choosing Your Horsehair

Horse manes and tails come in lots of different colors. Here's a general guide:

COAT COLOR	MANE AND TAIL COLOR
Black, brown, bay, buckskin	Black
Chestnut	Rusty red, pale yellow (flaxen), near black
Gray	Smoky, silvery, near white
Palomino	Cream or white
Pinto	Combination of white and brown or black

To make the mane and tail, you can use embroidery floss, yarn, string, or even raffia. It's really up to you. Here are some tips to help you make up your mind.

A. **Rayon embroidery floss** is an extra-glossy 6-ply thread that looks a bit flyaway when unraveled. This makes it a fun choice for a fancy mane and tail, such as the Arabian's.

B. **Cotton embroidery floss** is a slightly glossy 6-ply thread that can be easily unraveled to create full yet fine manes and tails, such as the Thoroughbred's.

C. **Medium-weight multi-ply cotton yarns** are soft and slightly fuzzy, and look wavy when unraveled. Perfect for extra-thick pony manes and tails.

D. **Pearl cotton** is a shiny, 2-ply thread that hangs straight and won't unravel; a good choice for the Morgan.

E. **Embroidery yarn** is a thicker alternative to floss and makes a good option for a heavy mane and tail, such as the Friesian's.

F. **Bulky, textured acrylic yarn** works well when creating fluffy manes and tails for foals, like those of the Clydesdales.

Making the Mane and Tail

The mane is created in sections that are glued side by side along the upper edge of the neck.

TO MAKE THE MANE

1 Cut a bunch of 6-inch pieces from the floss or yarn you've chosen. This length makes a mane that is fairly long, so you will have the option of keeping it like that or trimming it shorter.

2 Tie two or three pieces of the floss or yarn together with an overhand knot in the center to create one section of mane. Pull the knot very tight.

3 Unravel the individual strands on both sides of the knot.

4 Make enough sections to cover the neck from behind the ears down to the withers plus a couple of extra for the forelock. You'll probably need six to eight sections per inch of neck, depending on the type of floss or yarn and how thick you want the finished mane to be.

5 Set aside the mane sections while you make the tail.

TIP: If you plan on making a mane that's extra long or short, simply adjust the length of the pieces you cut in step 1. Just keep in mind that it's always a good idea to start a little longer than the length you're aiming for.

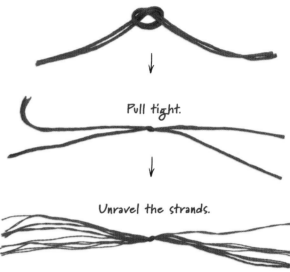

Tie with an overhand knot.

Pull tight.

Unravel the strands.

The tail can be as long as you like, but start with strands that are at least 11 inches long so you'll have extra to play with. You can always trim it shorter if you want.

TO MAKE THE TAIL

1 Cut 18 or more 11-inch pieces of the same floss or yarn you used for the mane.

2 Gather them in a bunch and tie another piece around the middle, pulling the knot tight.

3 Unravel the individual strands on both sides of the knot the way you did with the mane sections.

FACT: Appaloosas tend to have wispy manes and tails, whereas Friesians and Shetland Ponies have extra thick ones.

Tie your knot right in the middle of the strands.

Now it's time to attach the mane and tail to the horse. Start with one of the templates with its painted side down.

THE MANE

1 Start at the base of the neck (the withers). Stick a couple of glue dots close to the edge of the paper.

2 Arrange sections of mane side by side with the knots on top of the glue dots and the ends extending beyond the template.

3 Continue applying glue dots and adding sections of mane until you reach the top of the neck (the poll). (See Leave a Bridle Path on the next page.)

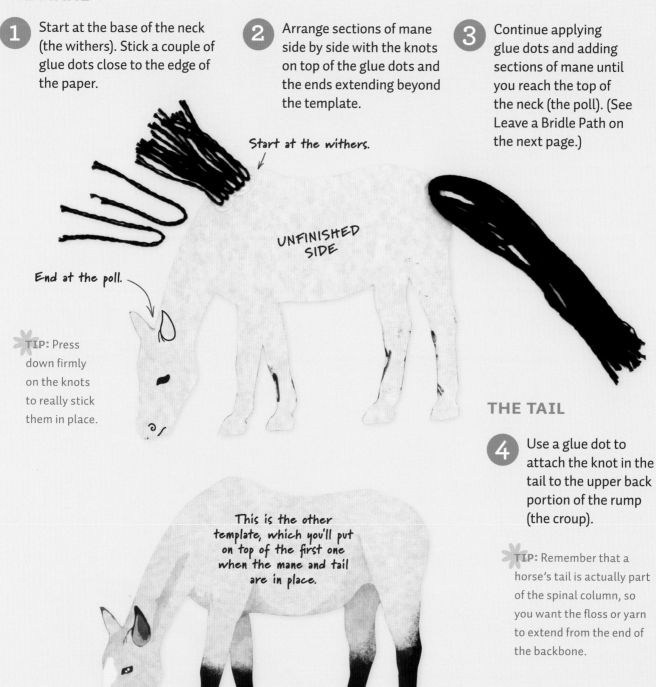

Start at the withers.

UNFINISHED SIDE

End at the poll.

TIP: Press down firmly on the knots to really stick them in place.

This is the other template, which you'll put on top of the first one when the mane and tail are in place.

THE TAIL

4 Use a glue dot to attach the knot in the tail to the upper back portion of the rump (the croup).

TIP: Remember that a horse's tail is actually part of the spinal column, so you want the floss or yarn to extend from the end of the backbone.

Fastening the Forelock

The forelock is the tuft of mane that falls between a horse's ears and helps protect its eyes from dust and bugs. There are two methods for attaching a forelock to a paper horse, depending on its profile.

A. FOR A HORSE WITH CLOSE-SET EARS

(Appaloosa, Friesian, Morgan, Saddlebred, Shetland Pony, Tennessee Walker, Thoroughbred)

1. Use scissors to make a small snip between the ears on **both** template pieces.

2. Stick a glue dot at the base of the ears on the **unpainted** side of each template.

3. Stick the knotted end of a mane section to each glue dot and then pull the floss or yarn down through the slit so that it falls on the painted side of the template. Don't worry about the length for now; you'll trim it short later.

Snip here.

glue dot

B. FOR A HORSE WITH WIDE-SPACED EARS

(Arabian, Clydesdale, Quarter Horse)

1. Glue a section of mane to the poll right at the base of the ear on the unpainted side of **both** template pieces.

2. After you glue the templates together (see page 35), gently pull this tuft of floss or yarn down onto the horse's forehead and use a dab of diluted glue to hold the strands in place.

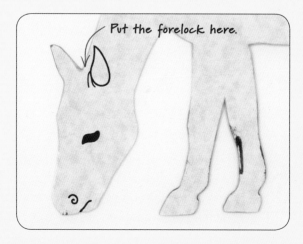

Put the forelock here.

Leave a Bridle Path

Because the crown of a bridle or halter fits right behind the ears, people often clip the mane at the top of the neck, or poll. To create a bridle path on a paper horse, simply leave a space between the forelock when attaching sections of mane. How long a space? With a horse that's ridden Western, the bridle path is usually as long as the ear is tall, whereas a horse that's ridden English tends to have a shorter one. With some breeds, such as the Saddlebred, the bridle path is extra long to show off the graceful arch of the horse's neck.

STEP 4. Finish Up

Now that you've attached the mane and tail, you can turn the painted templates into a finished horse equipped with stands for setting your paper model upright.

Making the Stands

Ready for some fancy footwork? Here's a little trick for using paper clips to make your finished horse stand up on its own. All you need are two paper clips, pliers, and a couple of glue dots.

TO MAKE THE STANDS

1 Use the pliers to bend the curved portion in the center of each paper clip straight up. It's important for the bend to be right at the point where the outer clip ends.

2 Wrap a glue dot around the upright portion of one stand.

3 Attach the stand to the **unpainted side of a back hoof** (choose the one that touches the ground when you set the template upright). The flat part of the clip should be right beneath the hoof.

4 Attach the **second stand to a front hoof**, again choosing the one that touches the ground.

*TIP: When you're attaching the paper clip stands and gluing the template pieces together, it's easier if you set down the template with the hooves lined up along the table edge. That way you can keep the bottoms of the paper clips flat without bending the horse's legs.

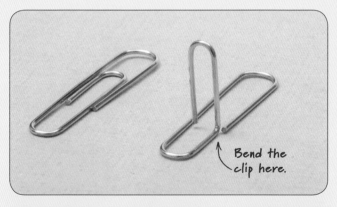

Bend the clip here.

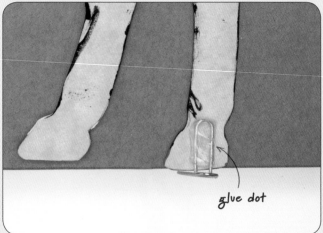

glue dot

Assembling Your Horse

Once the stands are attached, it's time to put the pieces together. You can use a quality glue stick or you can spread on tacky glue with a small or medium-size paintbrush.

TO GLUE THE PIECES TOGETHER

1 Spread glue on the entire unpainted side of the template. Don't skimp! Put on a good coat, even going over the mane and tail knots.

2 As soon as you finish, set the second template piece (with the painted side up) on top of the glued one, matching up all the edges as best you can. Firmly press the two pieces together.

3 Use pinch-style clothespins or large paper clips to hold the paper together at the tail, mane, ears, hooves, and any other spots that might separate while the glue dries.

4 Let the glue dry for several hours (overnight is best).

TIP: When applying glue, keep a damp paper towel nearby. It will come in handy for wiping your fingers if they get sticky or for dabbing away any glue that mistakenly ends up on the painted surface of the horse.

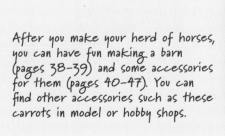

After you make your herd of horses, you can have fun making a barn (pages 38–39) and some accessories for them (pages 40–47). You can find other accessories such as these carrots in model or hobby shops.

Adjusting the Stands

After you remove the clothespins, stand up your horse. Ideally, both ends of the paper clip should touch the ground. If it seems a little wobbly, don't worry! You just need to adjust the stands by lowering the end that is sticking up. Before you do anything, here are two important things to remember:

* **Firmly pinch the lower leg and hoof** between your fingers to keep them from bending when you move the paper clip. You don't want to end up with a crease across the paper!

* Always **move the shorter end of the paper clip** because it is stronger and will hold its shape better when you make adjustments. If the longer end of the stand is sticking up, lift the short end a tiny bit. This will lower the long end. If the short end is sticking up, gently bend it down a bit.

Lift the short end to lower the long end.

TIP: Remember, you never need to move the long end of the clip when adjusting the stand, just the short end.

Touching Up

You're almost done! All that's left is a little grooming.

SEAL THE GAPS

Take a look at the edges of the paired-up templates for any spots that aren't well stuck together. Use a toothpick to insert tacky glue into any obvious gaps and pinch the paper together with your fingers or a pinch-style clothespin until it holds.

SPRUCE UP THE EDGES

Check for spots where the templates match up that might need a little touching up with paint. Likely areas are the edges of the paper where there are leg or facial markings, an Appaloosa blanket, and pinto patches.

Check the ears and hooves for enough glue.

Taming the Mane and Tail

Now's the time to decide whether you like the length of your horse's mane and tail or want to trim them. If you decide to go shorter, snip the strands separately so that the lengths vary ever so slightly. This will look much more realistic than if you cut the whole bunch straight across.

Braids, Bands, and Bangs

Horse manes and tails can be groomed in a number of ways. Here are a few options:

* Saddlebreds and other gaited breeds, as well as Friesians and Morgans usually have long, natural, flowing manes.

* Breeds such as the Thoroughbred and the Quarter Horse that are shown in English and Western classes tend to wear their manes shortened to 4 or so inches. For English events, the mane is often braided. On a Western horse, the mane is sometimes banded, meaning it is separated into sections and bound with colorful rubber bands to create a row of tiny ponytails.

* Jumpers and dressage horses may have banged tails. This means the bottom of the tail is cut straight across at the bottom, somewhere between the fetlock and the hock, to create a clean, even look. Western pleasure horses can have banged tails too, although they tend to be even longer.

Appaloosas often have a short and wispy mane.

A Thoroughbred's mane is usually worn short or braided.

Arabian manes are typically kept long and flowing.

Build a Tabletop Stable

This two-stall cardboard stable features a corrugated roof, Dutch doors, and an open back for easy access to the inside. It's a cinch to store away when you're not using it: Simply remove the roof, fold in the sides, and slide the flattened barn under a bed or behind a dresser.

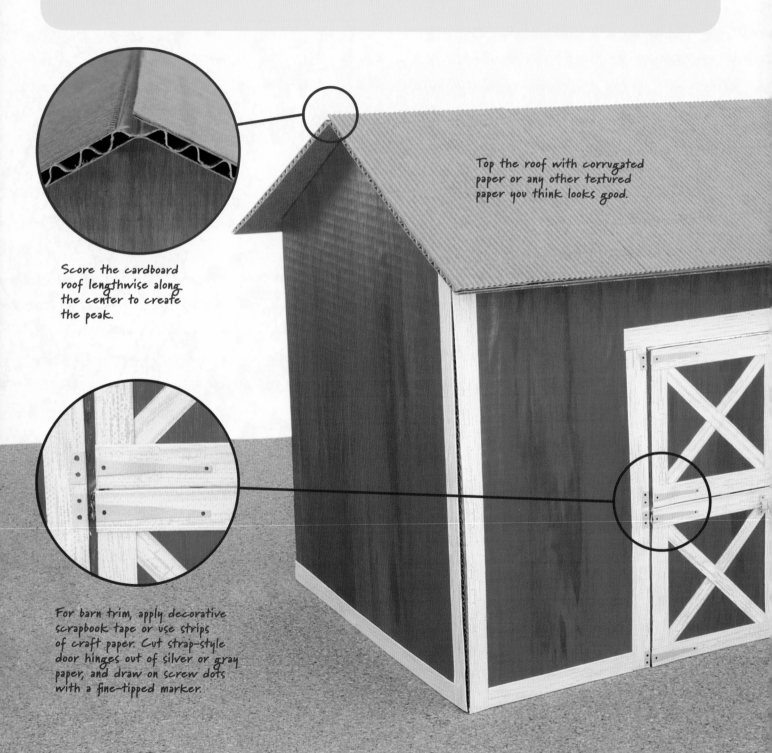

Top the roof with corrugated paper or any other textured paper you think looks good.

Score the cardboard roof lengthwise along the center to create the peak.

For barn trim, apply decorative scrapbook tape or use strips of craft paper. Cut strap-style door hinges out of silver or gray paper, and draw on screw dots with a fine-tipped marker.

TO CONSTRUCT A STABLE

Use this plan to cut the front and roof pieces out of cardboard. If you don't have enough cardboard in your home recycling bin, consider buying one of those science-project display boards. The dimensions work well for this stable plan.

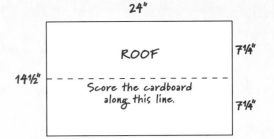

24"

ROOF

14½"

7¼"

7¼"

Score the cardboard along this line.

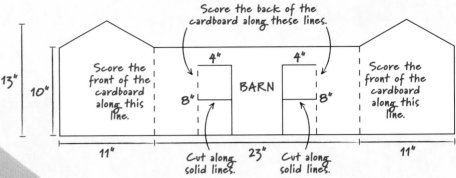

Score the back of the cardboard along these lines.

13"

10"

Score the front of the cardboard along this line.

4"

4"

BARN

8"

8"

Score the front of the cardboard along this line.

11"

Cut along solid lines.

23"

Cut along solid lines.

11"

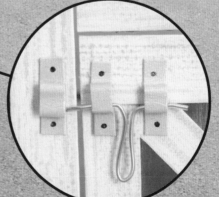

To keep the stall door open, insert a paper clip into the corrugation along the hinged edge.

Use flexible silver craft wire to shape a drop-style door latch. Attach it with hardware made from strips of silver or gray paper, and draw on screw dots.

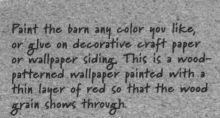

Paint the barn any color you like, or glue on decorative craft paper or wallpaper siding. This is a wood-patterned wallpaper painted with a thin layer of red so that the wood grain shows through.

Create Some Fun Horse Accessories

Once you've constructed a stable to settle your paper horses into, it's time to stock up on a few grooming supplies and other equine and barnyard accessories. You can even make some jumps and string up a colorful display of show ribbons.

Grooming Time

To keep your horses looking their best, you need a few tools and a box to keep them in.

SHEDDING BLADE

MATERIALS: Brown paper, silver or gray paper, regular scissors, scalloped-edge craft scissors, glue, toothpick

painted brush box

shedding blade

currycomb

barn bench

1 Cut out all the pieces.

Cut a straight-edged 1- by ¾-inch strip of brown paper, roll it into a small loop, and glue down the end.

Cut two ½-inch squares of brown paper and fold them in half to create handles.

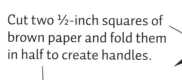

Cut a 3½- by ¼-inch strip of silver or gray paper for the blade. Use the scalloped scissors for one long side.

2 Glue the handles onto ends of the blade.

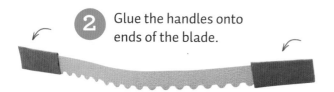

3 Slip the loop over one of the handles. Use a drop of glue applied with the tip of a toothpick to stick the loop to the outer (but not the inner) handle.

4 Slide the opposite handle through the loop.

PAINTED BRUSH BOX

MATERIALS: Template (see inside back cover), brown craft paper, regular scissors, a pushpin, a round toothpick, paint if desired

1 Photocopy the brush box template and use it as a pattern to cut the shape out of brown craft paper.

2 Clip the corners along the solid lines and fold along all the dotted lines. Use a pushpin to poke handle holes through the marks in the upper ends.

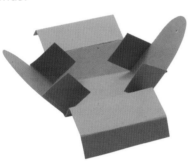

3 Fold in the ends of the brush box.

4 Fold the sides of the brush box up and over the end tabs and glue them in place, if needed.

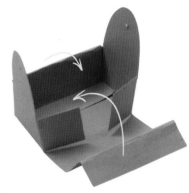

5 Use the tip of a toothpick to widen the handle holes.

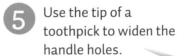

6 Snip off the tips of the toothpick and then thread it through the holes for the brush box handle.

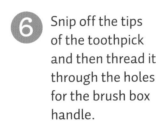

7 Paint the finished box if you like, sponging on darker patches for the final coat to create a weathered antique effect.

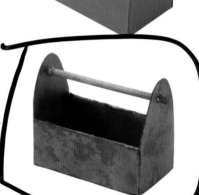

CURRYCOMB

MATERIALS: Black paper, red paper, regular scissors, scalloped-edge craft scissors, glue

1 Cut out all the pieces.

Cut a 4½- by ¼-inch strip of black paper. Use scalloped-edge craft scissors for one long side.

Cut two ¾-inch ovals of black paper for the top of the currycomb.

Cut a straight-edged 4¼- by ¼-inch strip of red paper for a handle.

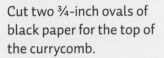

2 Roll the scalloped strip into a coil and use a glue dot to stick it to one of the ovals.

3 Wrap the red handle around the second oval, sticking the ends to the underneath.

4 Stick the two ovals together with the handle ends sandwiched between them.

BARN BENCH

MATERIALS: Skinny craft sticks, glue, sturdy scissors, paint (if desired)

1 Cut the skinny craft sticks into the following pieces:

* 4 inner legs
* 8 outer legs
* 6 side braces
* 2 seat cross braces
* 8 seat pieces

seat boards — 5¾" — ¼"

seat side brace — 5" — ¼"

leg cross brace — 1¾" — ¼"

seat cross brace — 1¾" — ¼"

inner leg — 1½" — ¼"

outer leg — 1¼" — ¼"

2 To make the bench legs, sandwich one inner leg between two outer legs and glue the pieces together.

3 Sandwich two leg tops between two leg cross braces and glue the pieces together. Repeat with the other pair of legs.

4 Glue the seat side braces to the ends of the leg cross braces.

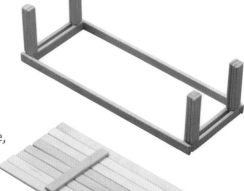

5 Arrange the seat boards side by side, then glue the two seat cross braces to them 1½ inches from the ends.

6 Glue the leg frame to the bottom of the bench.

Wait for the glue to dry before painting your bench any color you like.

Jumping Class

Here are a few ideas for setting up a show for your horses.

GROUND POLES/CAVALLETTI JUMPS

MATERIALS: One 8-inch wooden dowel and 8 mini wooden craft sticks for each cavalletti jump, white paint, blue paint (or other color), glue

1 Paint the 8-inch wooden dowels white.

2 Paint the mini wooden craft sticks blue.

3 Glue the craft sticks together in pairs to form Xs.

4 Glue one X on top of another to create a stand for each end of a dowel.

5 Set the stands upright and place the dowels on top.

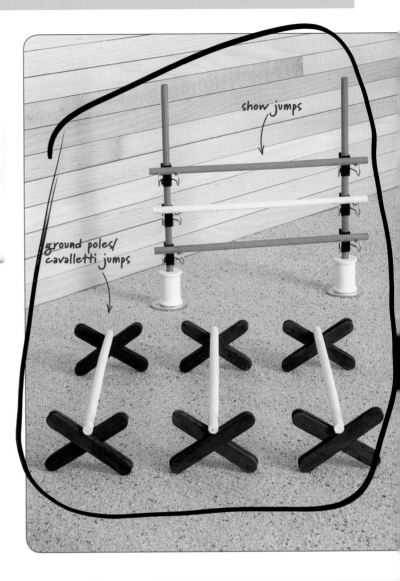

show jumps

ground poles/cavalletti jumps

SHOW JUMP

MATERIALS (for one jump): 2 wooden thread spools, 2 metal washers or coins, 5 (8-inch) wooden dowels, 6 small binder clips, paint

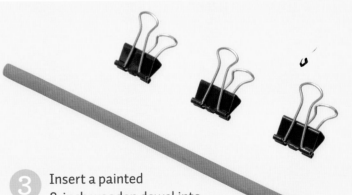

1 Paint the thread spools and dowels in your favorite colors.

2 To make each standard (vertical post), glue a spool onto a metal washer or coin base to weigh it down.

3 Insert a painted 8-inch wooden dowel into the center of each spool.

4 Attach binder clip "jump cups" to the dowels and set more painted dowels in place for poles.

Back at the Barn

When you get home from the show, you'll want to string up your ribbons and reward your horse with an extra-full hay bag.

SHOW RIBBONS

MATERIALS: Colored paper (shades of blue, red, yellow), glue, soft craft wire, tiny "gems" (optional)

1 For each ribbon, cut three strips of paper approximately 1½ inch by ¼ inch; two ½-inch circles; and one ⅜-inch circle.

2 To make the rosette, glue the ⅜-inch paper circle onto a ½-inch circle and cut decorative notches around the edge. If you want, stick a faux gem to the center.

3 Glue a U-shaped piece of soft craft wire and the three paper ribbons to another ½-inch circle.

4 Glue the rosette onto the ribbon.

5 Bend the wire down against the back of the ribbon to form a hook.

HAY BAG

MATERIALS: Small plastic mesh bag (the kind chocolate coins come in), embroidery floss or heavy thread, needle, scissors, some hay (bits of real hay, straw, or raffia)

1 Snip off the top section of the mesh bag.

2 Fold over the cut edge and thread about 8 inches of embroidery floss or string through the folded mesh all the way around the top. Remove the needle and knot the thread ends together, trimming as necessary.

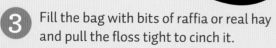

3 Fill the bag with bits of raffia or real hay and pull the floss tight to cinch it.

HAY-BAG HANGER

MATERIALS: Gray or silver paper, push-pin, fine-tipped marker, scissors, jewelry jump ring, soft craft wire, glue dot

1 Cut two ¾-inch squares from gray or silver paper. On one of them, draw screw dots in the corners and use a pushpin to poke a pair of holes in the center.

2 Slip a jewelry jump ring onto the center of a U-shaped piece of soft craft wire.

3 Thread the craft wire through the holes and bend the ends against the back of the square.

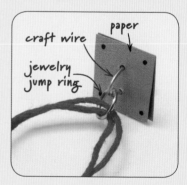

craft wire
paper
jewelry jump ring

4 Use a glue dot to stick the second square to the back of the first, covering the ends of the craft wire.

5 Stick the holder to the barn siding with a glue dot and thread the hay-bag string through the ring.

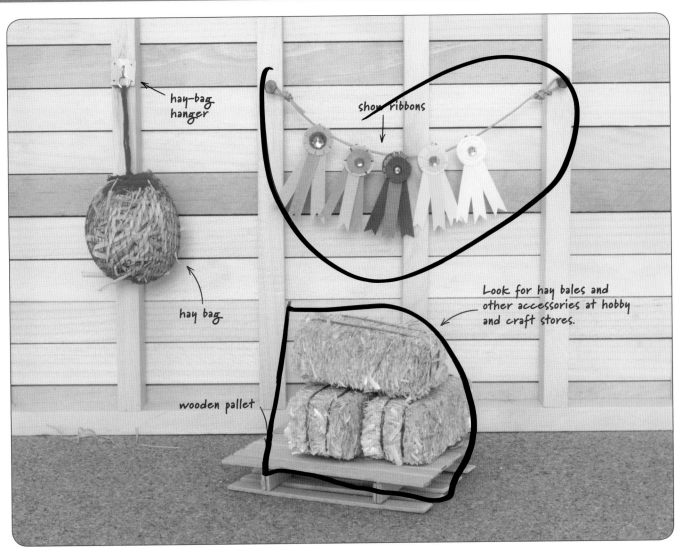

hay-bag
hanger

show ribbons

hay bag

Look for hay bales and
other accessories at hobby
and craft stores.

wooden pallet

WOODEN PALLET

MATERIALS: Wooden craft sticks, glue,
sturdy scissors

1 Cut wooden craft sticks as follows:
* Four 3-inch lengths for cross braces
* Twelve 4-inch lengths for slats

2 Glue together two of the 3-inch pieces to make a cross
brace. Make a second brace just like it.

3 Arrange five of the slats slightly apart and glue the
narrow edges of the two cross braces on top, slightly
in from the ends of the slats. Let the glue dry.

4 Glue the remaining seven slats on top, spacing them
closer together than the bottom ones.

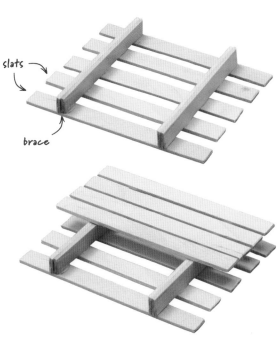

slats

brace

Time to Tack Up

Here a few pieces of tack you can make for your horses. Let your imagination go and create your own saddles, blankets, and other equipment!

two-loop halter

halter with cheek straps

lead line

longe line

LONGE LINE

MATERIALS: 1 jewelry jump ring, a lobster claw clasp with chain extension, 24-inch length of suede jewelry cord (thin ribbon also works), 6-inch length of embroidery floss or thread, glue

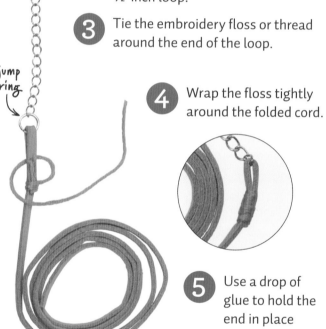

jump ring

1 Attach the jewelry jump ring to the end of the chain.

2 Thread the end of the cord through the jump ring and fold it to form a ½-inch loop.

3 Tie the embroidery floss or thread around the end of the loop.

4 Wrap the floss tightly around the folded cord.

5 Use a drop of glue to hold the end in place

Let's Longe

Longeing (pronounced lunge-ing) is a form of exercising and/or training a horse without actually riding it. The trainer clips a 30-foot-long line to the halter or bridle and the horse moves in a large circle around him or her. This is also a great way to loosen a horse's stiff muscles or safely calm a nervous or energetic horse by putting him through his paces until he settles down.

TWO-LOOP HALTER

MATERIALS: colored craft paper (quilling paper works great), glue, 3 small jewelry jump rings

1 Cut three strips of paper as follows:
* one ⅛ inch by 1 inch
* one ⅛ inch by 2¼ inches
* one ⅛ inch by 4½ inches

2 Use the 1-inch strip to form a ¾-inch circle for the noseband; glue the ends together.

3 Make a connecting strap by folding the 2¼-strip at the 1-inch mark and slipping on a jewelry jump ring.

1"

1¼"

4 Slip the connecting strap over the noseband so that the ring is just below it. Glue down the 1-inch strap end.

Glue here.

5 Make a crownpiece/throatlatch strap by folding the 4½-inch strip at the ½-inch mark, slipping on two jewelry jump rings and gluing down the strap end.

Glue here.

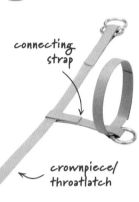

6 Fold the back of the connecting strap over the crownpiece/throatlatch and glue down the very end, forming a loop that allows the longer strap to slide from side to side. This will let you adjust the halter when it's on the horse.

connecting strap

crownpiece/throatlatch

7 To fasten the finished halter, thread the end of the crownpiece strap through both throatlatch rings, then over the outer ring and back through the under ring.

✳ **TIP:** For an even fancier halter, like the red one worn by the Tennessee Walker on page 4, connect the noseband to the crownpiece with a pair of cheek straps.

LEAD ROPE

MATERIALS: A jewelry jump ring, a lobster claw clasp, thin yarn or cord (two different colors is nice)

1 Attach the jewelry jump ring to the lobster claw clasp

2 Thread 16-inch strands of yarn or thin cord through the ring.

3 Braid the yarn — a barrel braid, with four strands, looks especially good — and knot the end.

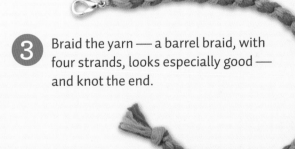

DEDICATION

*To Ginger, Shadow, Silverbird, Shot Gun, Nizzar, Lyric, Sassy, Bid, Grubby,
and all the other horses and ponies I've had the pleasure to ride or drive.
Special thanks, too, to my wonderful childhood Silver Spurs 4-H Club
leader, Mrs. Jones, for teaching me and my fellow club members
what an honor and joy it is to be part of the equine world.*

The mission of Storey Publishing is to serve our customers by
publishing practical information that encourages
personal independence in harmony with the environment.

Edited by Lisa H. Hiley and Deborah Burns
Art direction and book design by Jessica Armstrong
Cover design by Philip E. Pascuzzo
Text production by Sourena Parham

Photography by © Mark Mantegna, except for back cover and pages 29, 30, 35, and 36 by Mars Vilaubi
Photo styling by Cindy A. Littlefield

*Special thanks to Jade Littlefield for her help refining the templates and completing
the painting and shading, and to Kevin Ayer, who designed the miniature barn bench
and built the barn and fencing backdrops in the photos.*

Storey Publishing
210 MASS MoCA Way
North Adams, MA 01247
www.storey.com

Printed in China by R.R. Donnelley
10   9   8   7   6   5   4   3   2   1

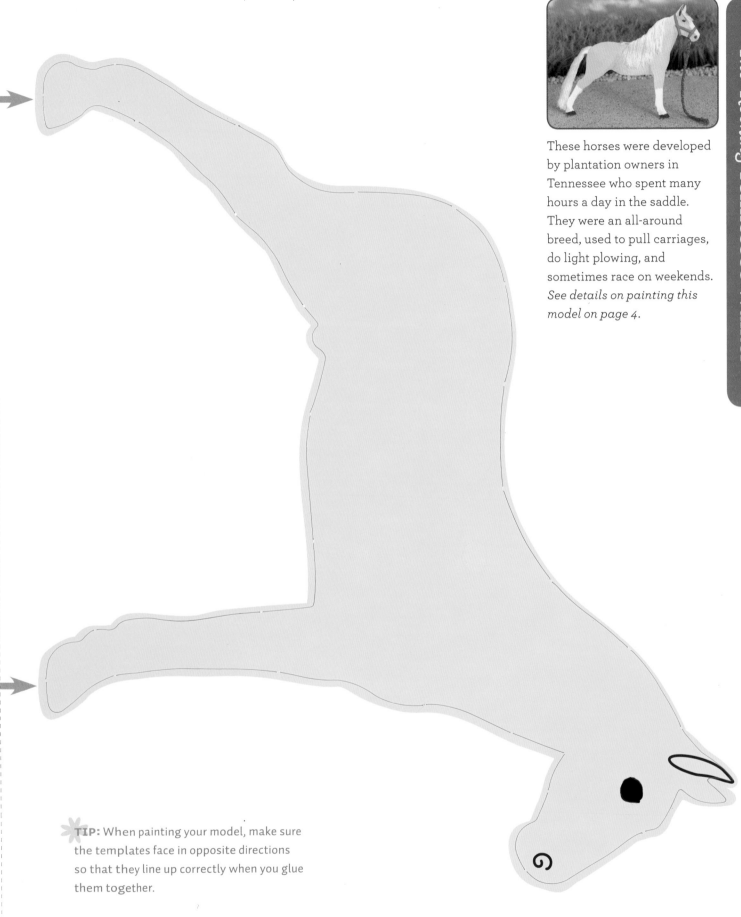

These horses were developed by plantation owners in Tennessee who spent many hours a day in the saddle. They were an all-around breed, used to pull carriages, do light plowing, and sometimes race on weekends. *See details on painting this model on page 4.*

✳ **TIP:** When painting your model, make sure the templates face in opposite directions so that they line up correctly when you glue them together.

NOTE: *Be extra careful around the legs when punching out the templates. The arrows show where to place the paper clip stands.*

49

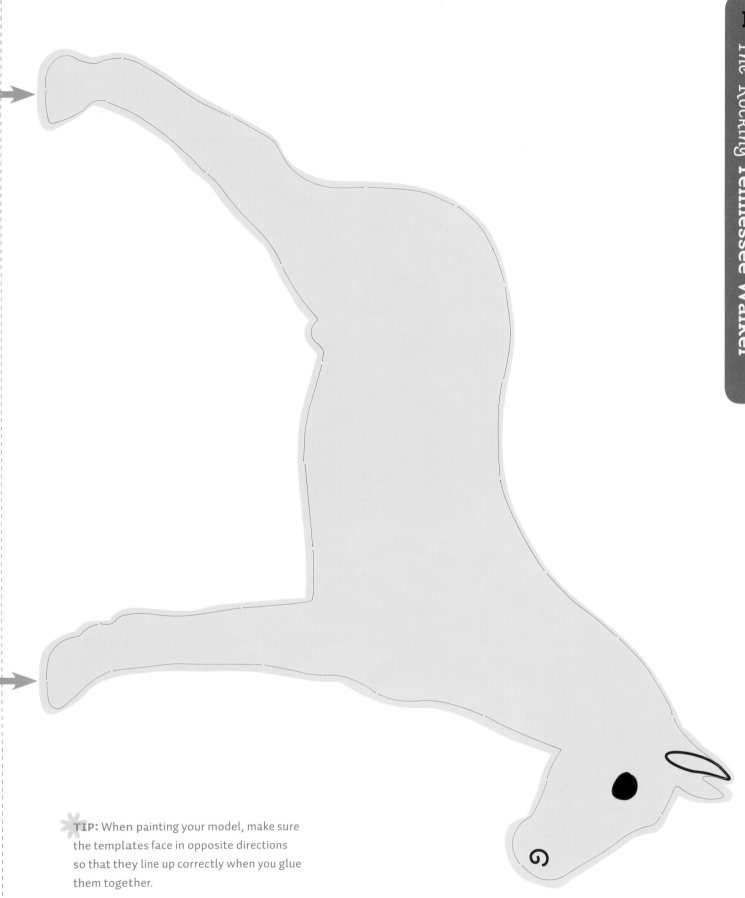

TIP: When painting your model, make sure the templates face in opposite directions so that they line up correctly when you glue them together.

NOTE: *Be extra careful around the legs when punching out the templates.*
The arrows show where to place the paper clip stands.

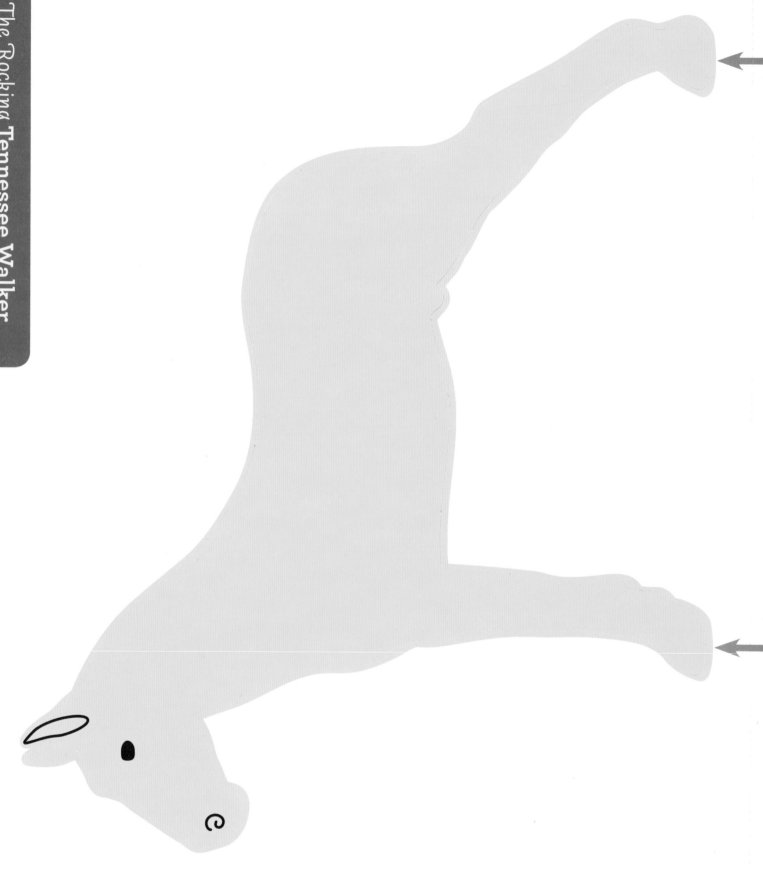

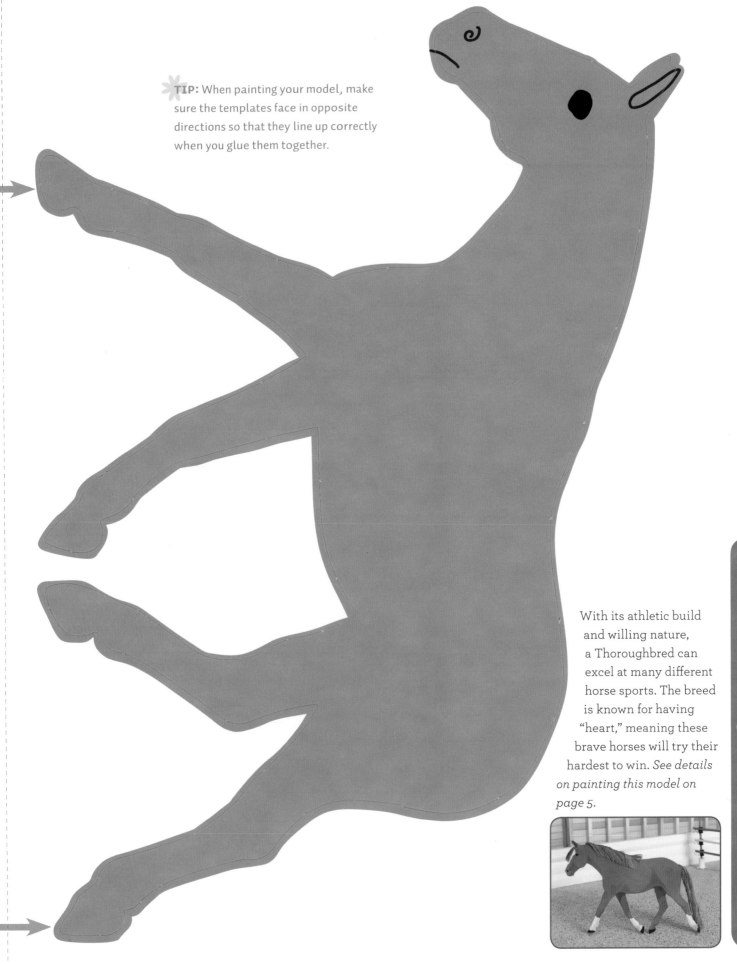

TIP: When painting your model, make sure the templates face in opposite directions so that they line up correctly when you glue them together.

With its athletic build and willing nature, a Thoroughbred can excel at many different horse sports. The breed is known for having "heart," meaning these brave horses will try their hardest to win. *See details on painting this model on page 5.*

See details on painting this model on page 5.

NOTE: *Be extra careful around the legs when punching out the templates. The arrows show where to place the paper clip stands.*

A The Thundering Thoroughbred

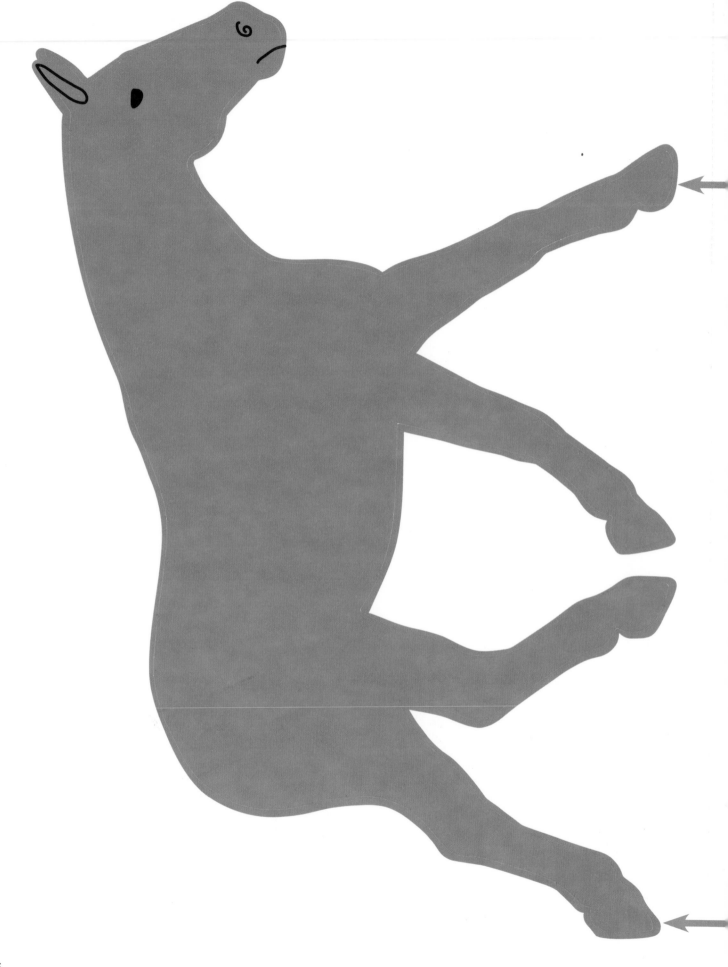

The Thundering Thoroughbred

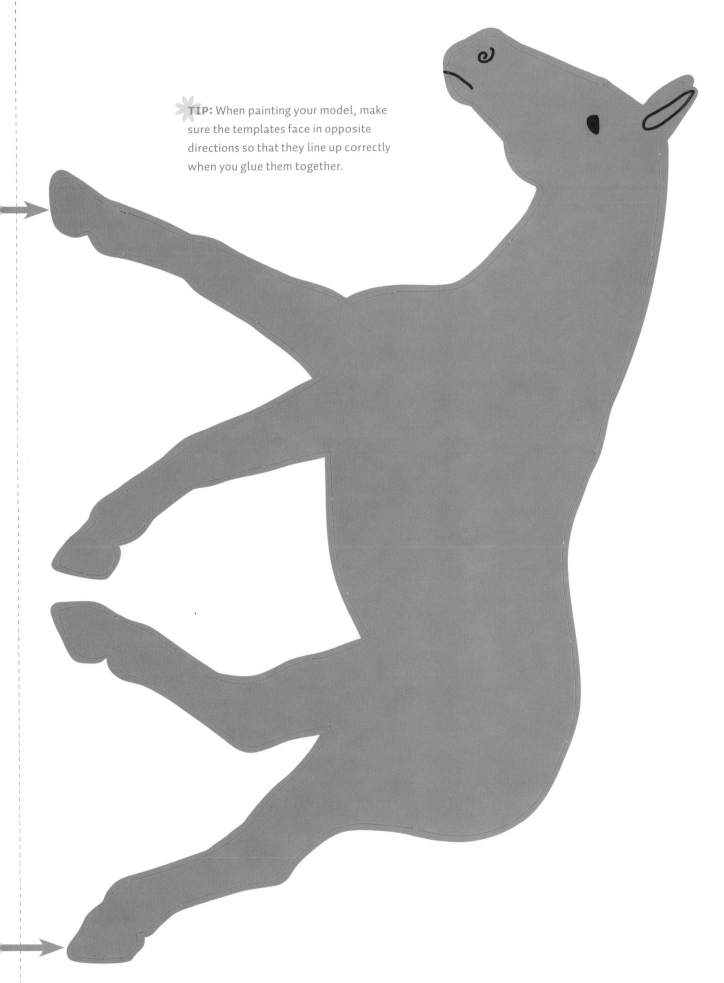

TIP: When painting your model, make sure the templates face in opposite directions so that they line up correctly when you glue them together.

NOTE: *Be extra careful around the legs when punching out the templates.*
The arrows show where to place the paper clip stands.

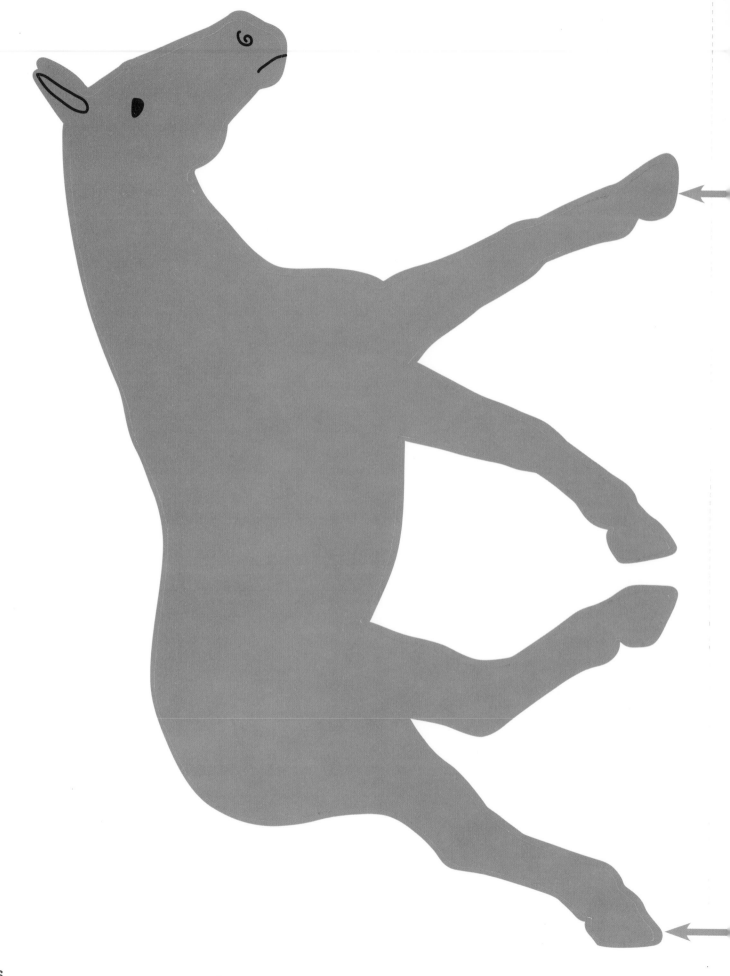

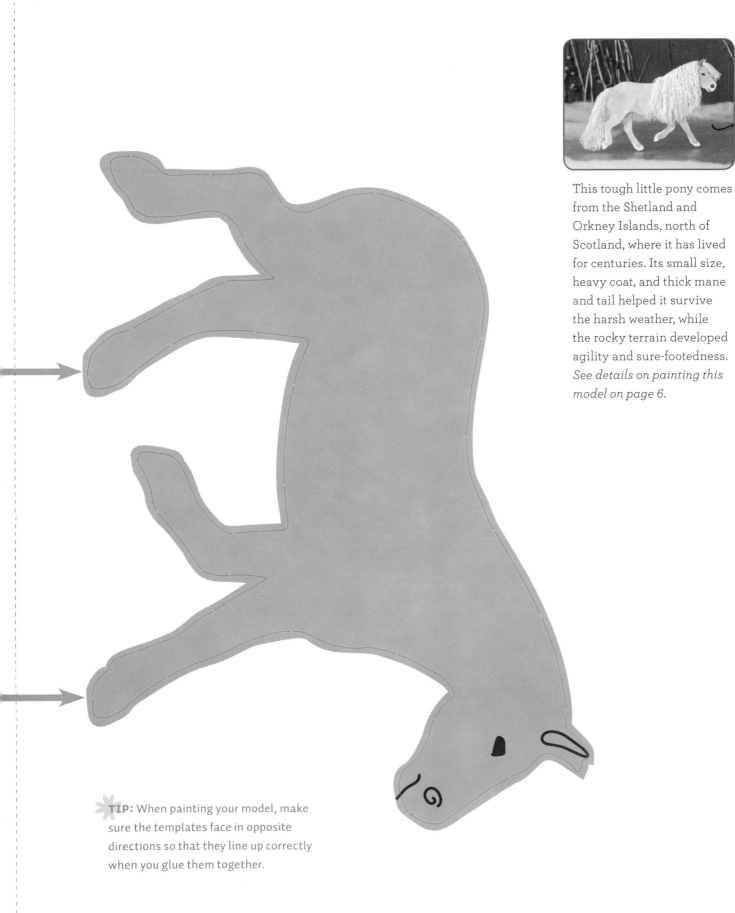

This tough little pony comes from the Shetland and Orkney Islands, north of Scotland, where it has lived for centuries. Its small size, heavy coat, and thick mane and tail helped it survive the harsh weather, while the rocky terrain developed agility and sure-footedness. *See details on painting this model on page 6.*

TIP: When painting your model, make sure the templates face in opposite directions so that they line up correctly when you glue them together.

NOTE: *Be extra careful around the legs when punching out the templates. The arrows show where to place the paper clip stands.*

57

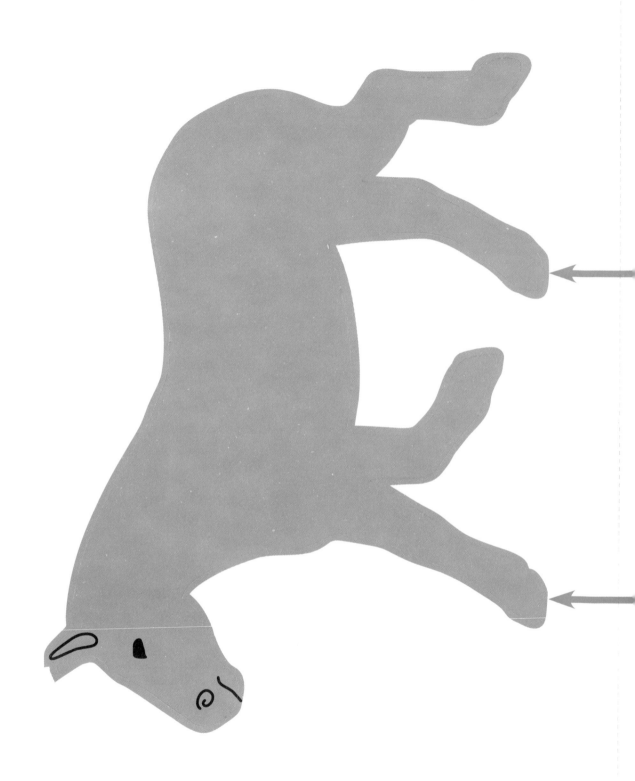

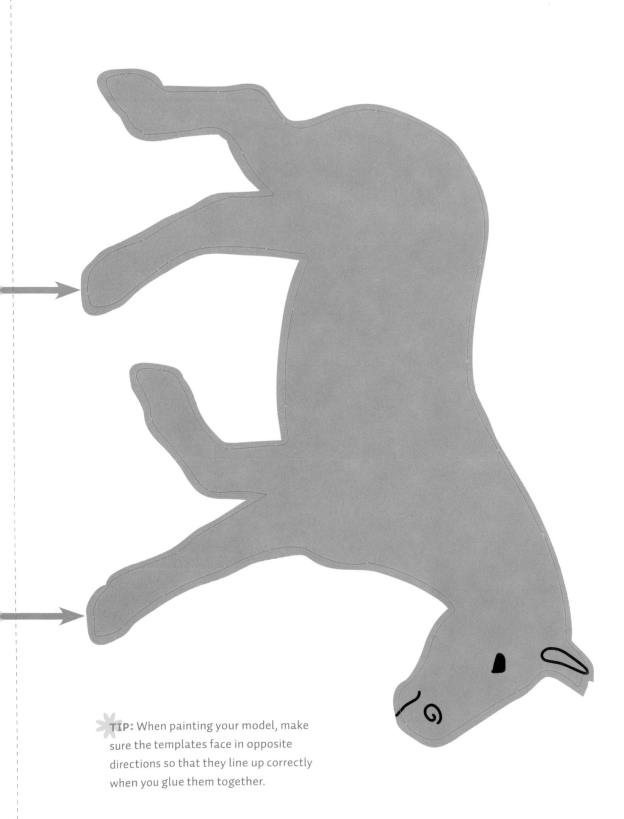

TIP: When painting your model, make sure the templates face in opposite directions so that they line up correctly when you glue them together.

NOTE: *Be extra careful around the legs when punching out the templates. The arrows show where to place the paper clip stands.*

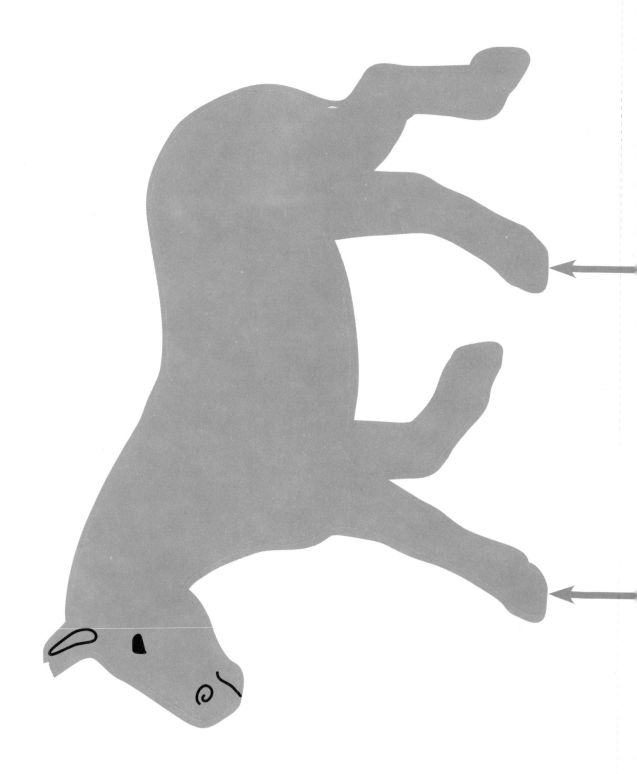

✳ TIP: When painting your model, make sure the templates face in opposite directions so that they line up correctly when you glue them together.

The Morgan is a versatile horse, which means it can do many things well, including farmwork, showing, trail riding, and even herding cattle. It was popular as a cavalry horse and is often used by mounted police. *See details on painting this model on page 7.*

A

The Mighty Morgan

NOTE: *Be extra careful around the legs when punching out the templates.*
➤ *The arrows show where to place the paper clip stands.*

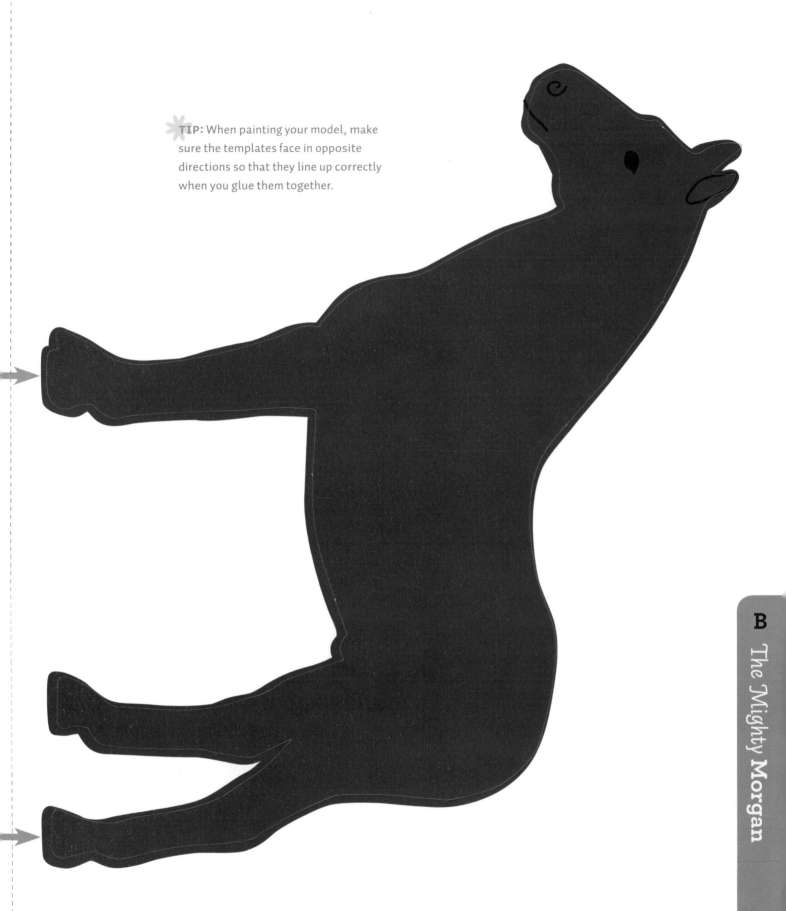

TIP: When painting your model, make sure the templates face in opposite directions so that they line up correctly when you glue them together.

NOTE: *Be extra careful around the legs when punching out the templates. The arrows show where to place the paper clip stands.*

The Friesian is a strikingly beautiful horse with an exceptionally full mane and tail. It is never permitted to dock (cut short) a Friesian's tail and even trimming the mane, tail, and fetlock hair is discouraged. Some Friesians' manes grow almost to the ground! *See details on painting this model on page 8.*

TIP: When painting your model, make sure the templates face in opposite directions so that they line up correctly when you glue them together.

NOTE: *Be extra careful around the legs when punching out the templates.*
The arrows show where to place the paper clip stands.

TIP: When painting your model, make sure the templates face in opposite directions so that they line up correctly when you glue them together.

NOTE: *Be extra careful around the legs when punching out the templates. The arrows show where to place the paper clip stands.*

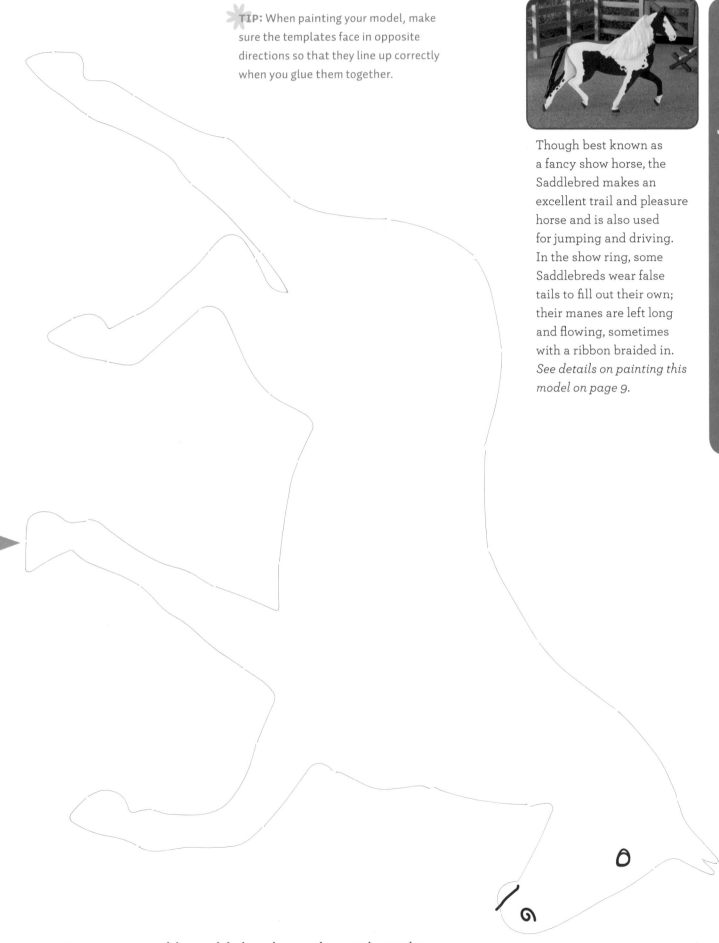

TIP: When painting your model, make sure the templates face in opposite directions so that they line up correctly when you glue them together.

Though best known as a fancy show horse, the Saddlebred makes an excellent trail and pleasure horse and is also used for jumping and driving. In the show ring, some Saddlebreds wear false tails to fill out their own; their manes are left long and flowing, sometimes with a ribbon braided in. *See details on painting this model on page 9.*

NOTE: *Be extra careful around the legs when punching out the templates. The arrows show where to place the paper clip stands.*

69

TIP: When painting your model, make sure the templates face in opposite directions so that they line up correctly when you glue them together.

NOTE: *Be extra careful around the legs when punching out the templates.*
The arrows show where to place the paper clip stands.

TIP: When painting your model, make sure the templates face in opposite directions so that they line up correctly when you glue them together.

Named for its speed at the sprint, a Quarter Horse can beat a Thoroughbred over a short distance. The most popular breed in the world, the Quarter Horse isn't just a ranch and rodeo horse but can also perform well in racing, jumping, and dressage. *See details on painting this model on page 10.*

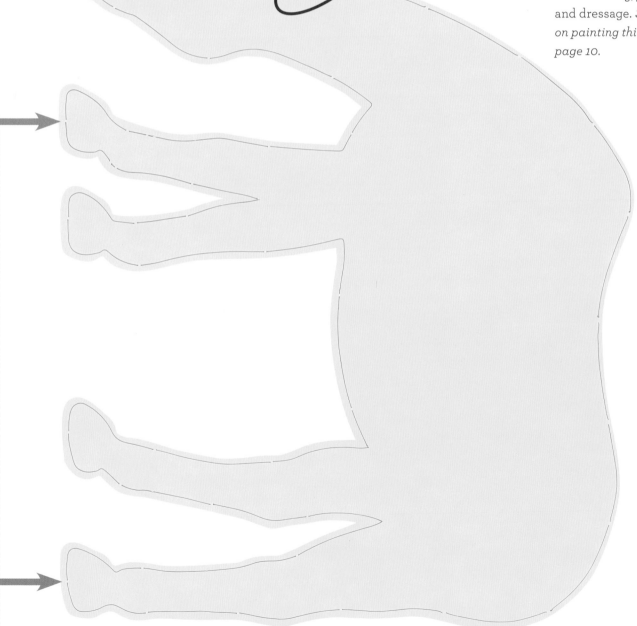

NOTE: *Be extra careful around the legs when punching out the templates.*
The arrows show where to place the paper clip stands.

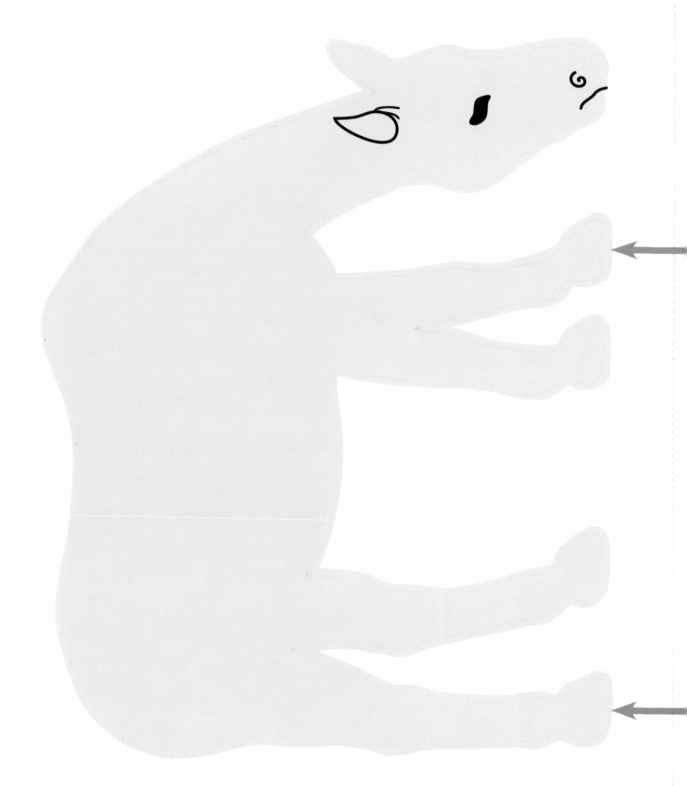

TIP: When painting your model, make sure the templates face in opposite directions so that they line up correctly when you glue them together.

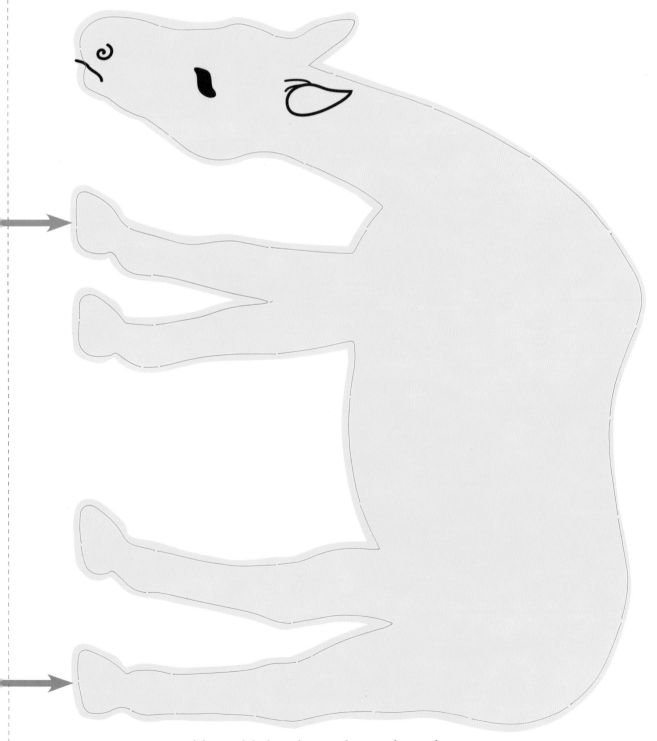

NOTE: *Be extra careful around the legs when punching out the templates.*
The arrows show where to place the paper clip stands.

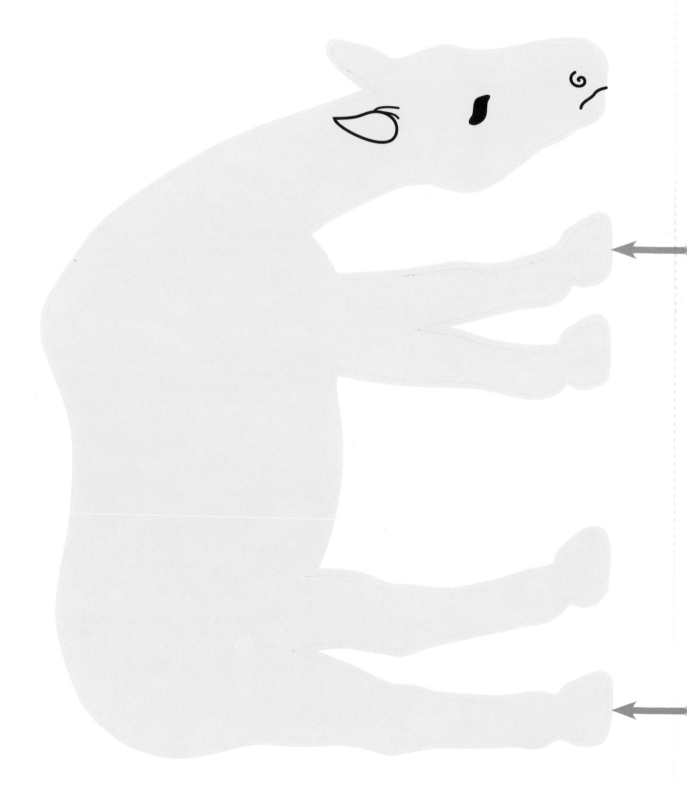

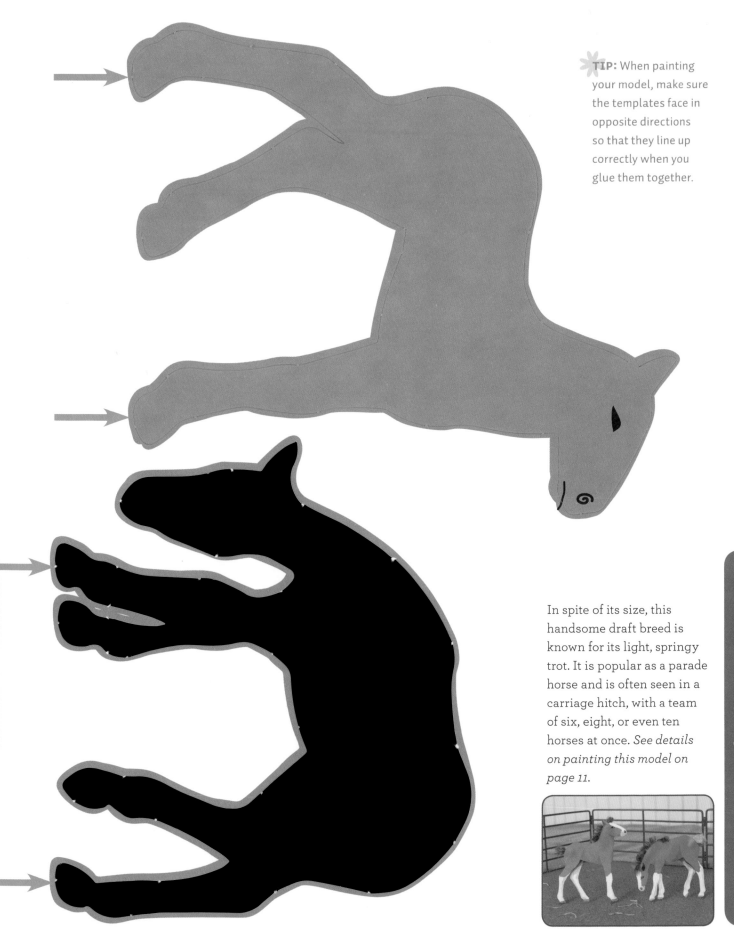

TIP: When painting your model, make sure the templates face in opposite directions so that they line up correctly when you glue them together.

In spite of its size, this handsome draft breed is known for its light, springy trot. It is popular as a parade horse and is often seen in a carriage hitch, with a team of six, eight, or even ten horses at once. *See details on painting this model on page 11.*

NOTE: *Be extra careful around the legs when punching out the templates.* The arrows show where to place the paper clip stands.

77

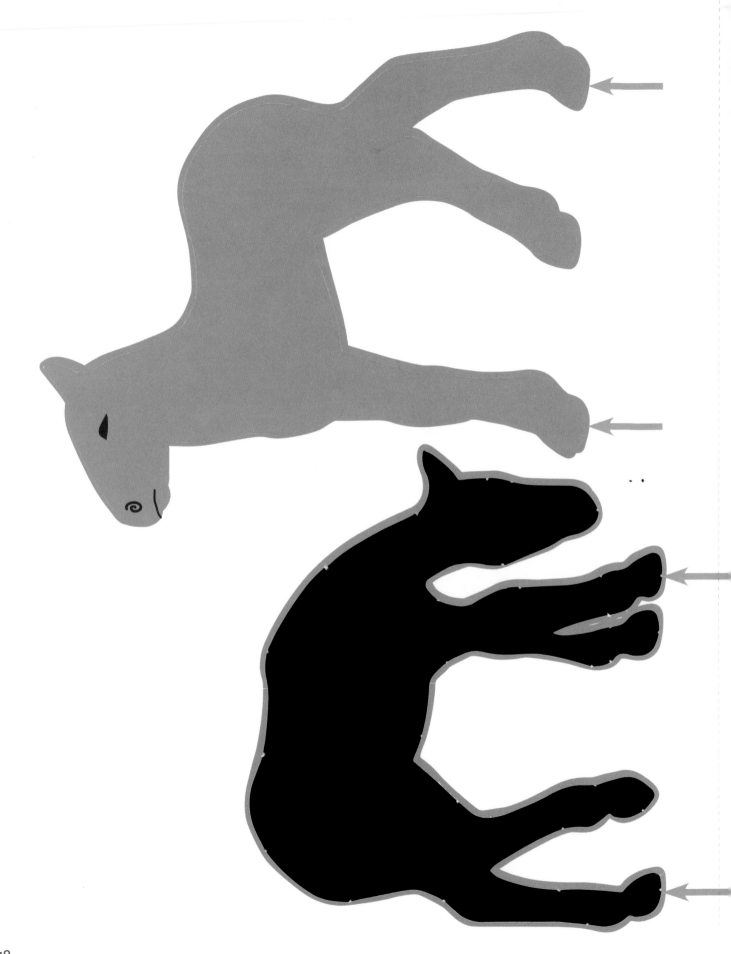

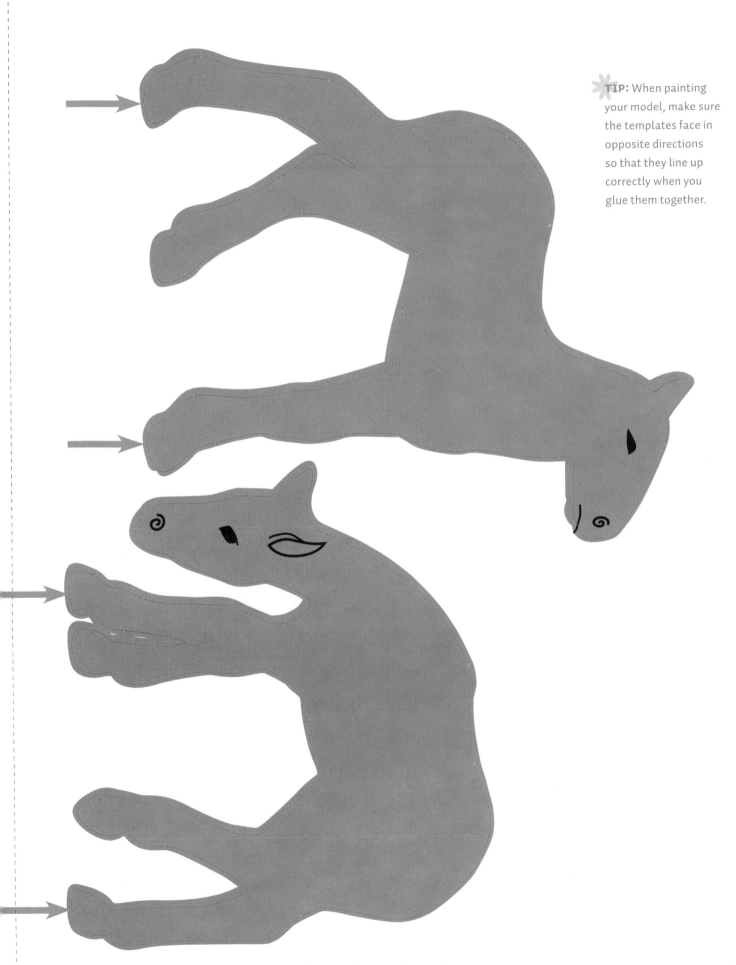

NOTE: *Be extra careful around the legs when punching out the templates.*
➡ *The arrows show where to place the paper clip stands.*

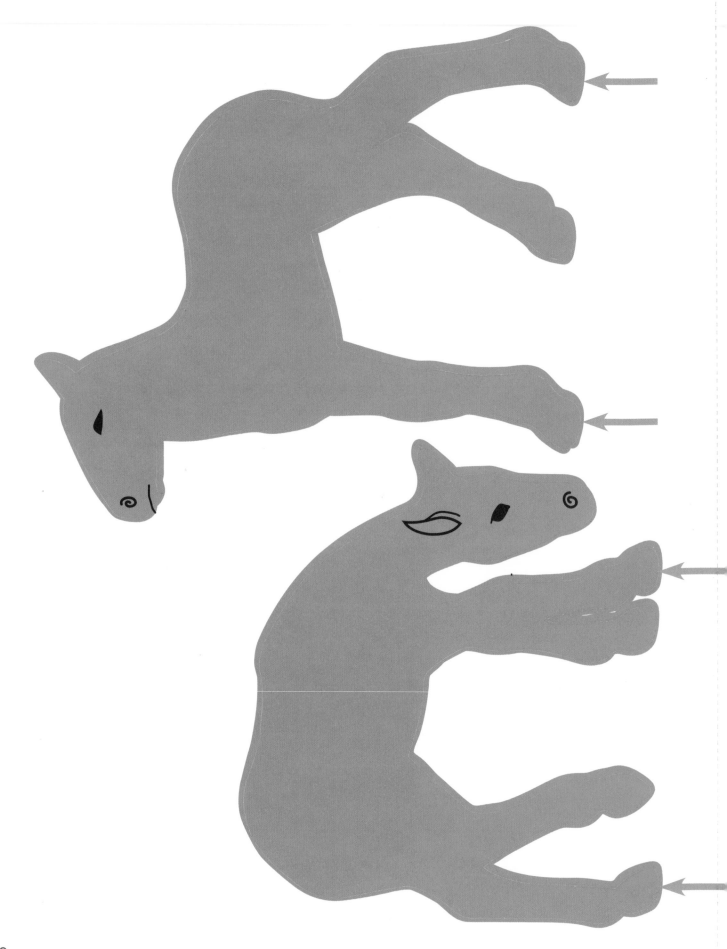

TIP: When painting your model, make sure the templates face in opposite directions so that they line up correctly when you glue them together.

The Nez Percé Indians lived near the Palouse River, so their horses became known as "Palouse horses" and then "Palouseys," which turned into "Appaloosas." In addition to a blanket of spots, Appy patterns include leopard spots (dark spots on a light coat) and snowflake (white spots on a dark coat). *See details on painting this model on page 12.*

NOTE: *Be extra careful around the legs when punching out the templates. The arrows show where to place the paper clip stands.*

*TIP: When painting your model, make sure the templates face in opposite directions so that they line up correctly when you glue them together.

NOTE: *Be extra careful around the legs when punching out the templates. The arrows show where to place the paper clip stands.*

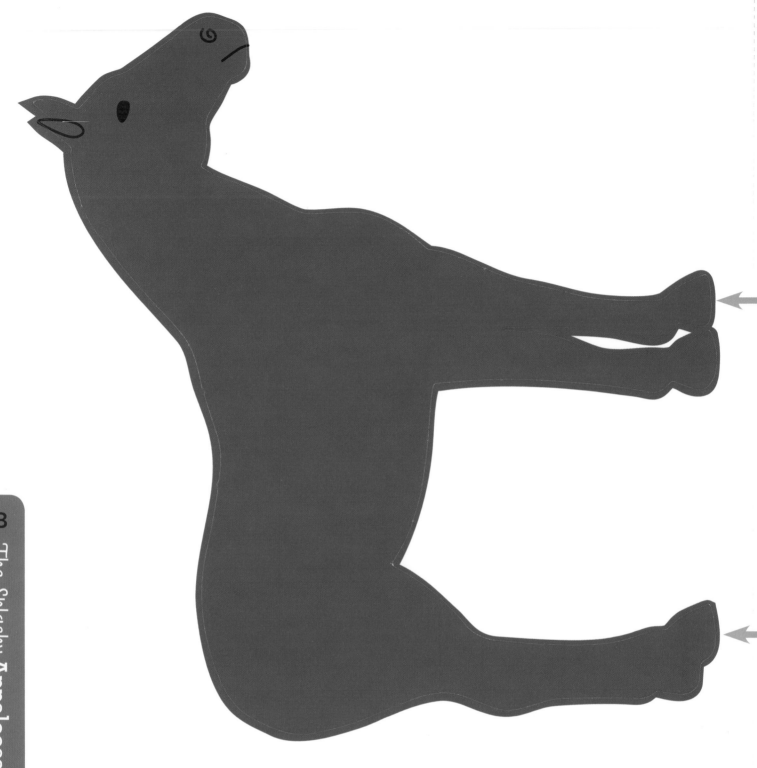

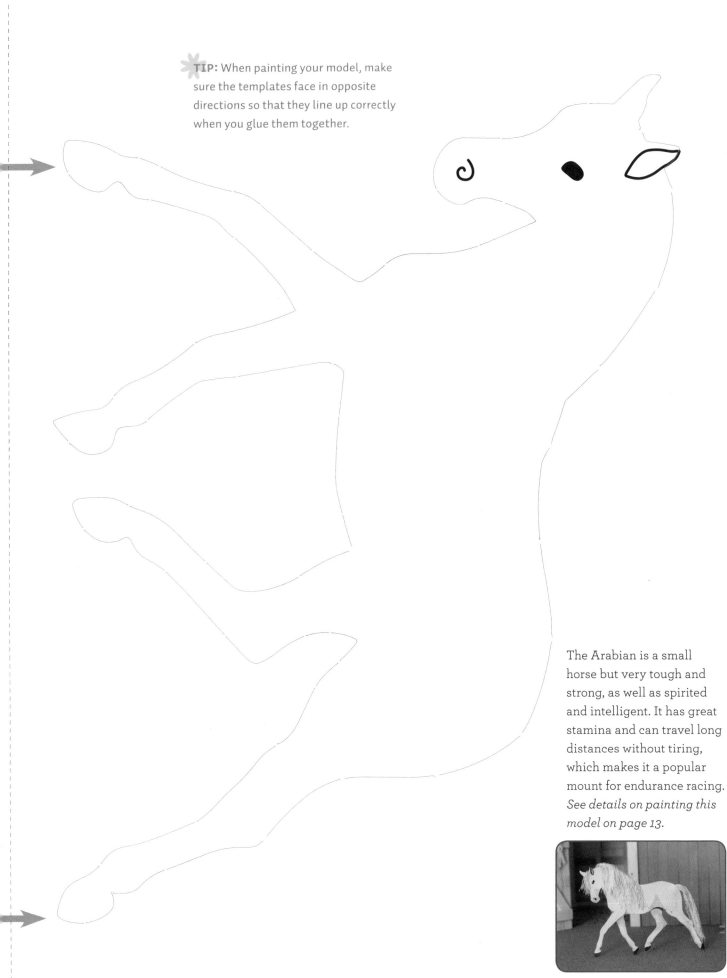

TIP: When painting your model, make sure the templates face in opposite directions so that they line up correctly when you glue them together.

A

The Elegant **Arabian**

The Arabian is a small horse but very tough and strong, as well as spirited and intelligent. It has great stamina and can travel long distances without tiring, which makes it a popular mount for endurance racing. *See details on painting this model on page 13.*

NOTE: *Be extra careful around the legs when punching out the templates. The arrows show where to place the paper clip stands.*

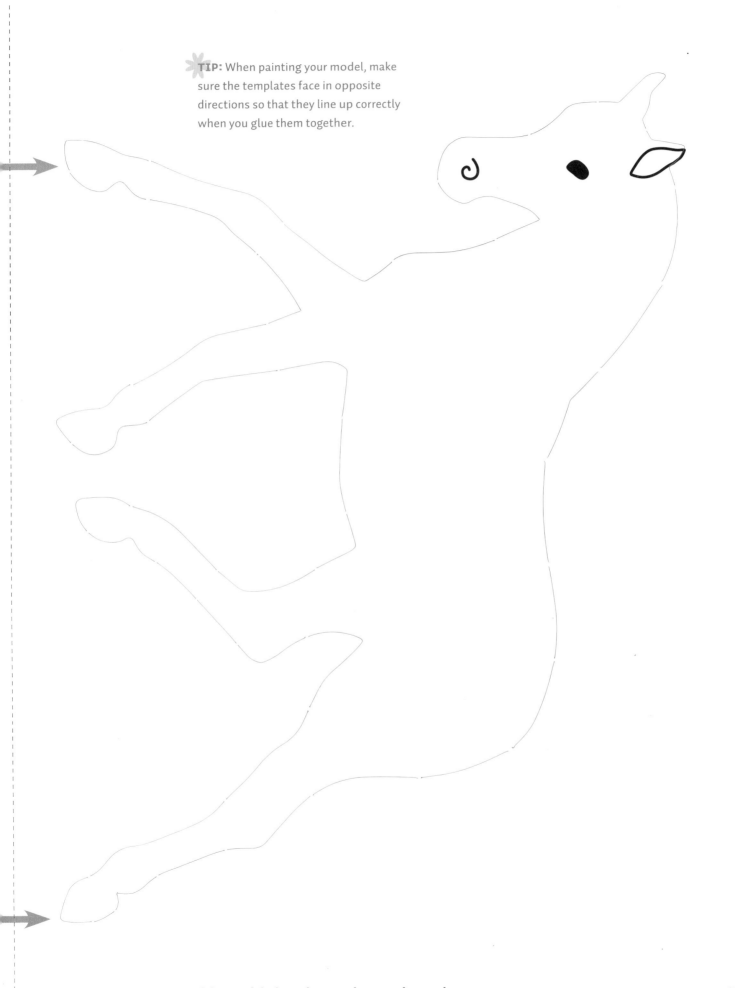

TIP: When painting your model, make sure the templates face in opposite directions so that they line up correctly when you glue them together.

NOTE: *Be extra careful around the legs when punching out the templates. The arrows show where to place the paper clip stands.*